Olexander Scherba

Ukraine vs. Darkness

Undiplomatic Thoughts

With a foreword by Adrian Karatnycky

"If you really want to make sense of what is happening in Ukraine today, and how Europe views what is going on in Ukraine, read this book."

Ivan Krastev, author of *Democracy Disrupted* and *After Europe*

"A government insider's gripping and incisive look at Ukraine and its war with Russia. Essential for anyone who wants to understand this poorly known country, whose fate is pivotal for the future of Europe and the global balance of power."

Peter Pomerantsev, author of *Nothing Is True and Everything Is Possible* and *This Is Not Propaganda*

"From one of Ukraine's leading diplomats, these unvarnished "undiplomatic thoughts" are deeply personal reflections on a country on the front lines of liberal democracy's civilizational battle against kleptocratic authoritarianism. Scherba expertly deconstructs myths about Ukraine, as well as Russian motives in his country, eloquently voicing its people's aspirations to determine their own future by escaping the Kremlin's shadow and becoming a full-fledged European country."

Gregory Feifer, author of *Russians* and *The Great Gamble*

"Ambassador Olexander Scherba's book is an excellent and instructive example of how patriotism can draw upon the foundations of Christian humanism while avoiding the trap of nationalism."

Anton Shekhovtsov, author of
Russia and the Western Far Right: Tango Noir

"In his book, Olexander Scherba avoids the usual stereotypes of a diplomat as a frozen bureaucrat and of a post-Soviet Ukrainian having difficulty speaking to the world. He himself is proof of Ukraine's fight against darkness."

Myroslav Marynovych,
vice-rector of Ukrainian Catholic University in Lviv

Olexander Scherba

UKRAINE VS. DARKNESS

Undiplomatic Thoughts

With a foreword by Adrian Karatnycky

ibidem
Verlag

Bibliographic information published by the Deutsche Nationalbibliothek
Die Deutsche Nationalbibliothek lists this publication in the Deutsche Nationalbibliografie; detailed bibliographic data are available in the Internet at http://dnb.d-nb.de.

Bibliografische Information der Deutschen Nationalbibliothek
Die Deutsche Nationalbibliothek verzeichnet diese Publikation in der Deutschen Nationalbibliografie; detaillierte bibliografische Daten sind im Internet über http://dnb.d-nb.de abrufbar.

ISBN-13: 978-3-8382-1501-3
© *ibidem*-Verlag, Stuttgart 2021

Printed in the United States of America

Contents

Foreword

by Adrian Karatnycky

Ambassador Olexander Scherba's book of essays is an important means by which to understand the nature of Ukraine's struggle for sovereignty. It is a window into Russian hybrid war. And it is a thoughtful look at Ukraine's frequently arcane and always complex politics, in which the Russian factor and Russian fifth columns loom large.

From his vantage point of diplomatic service in Vienna, as well as his past service in Bonn, Berlin and Washington, Scherba is a sophisticated and congenial guide to Ukraine and its crucial place in the complex geopolitics of East Central Europe. In a fair-minded and illuminating fashion, he discusses the phenomena of civil society, of religion, of nationalism, and of reform in his own country. He takes on major issues and challenges in international affairs, including Russian imperialism, hybrid war, and the future of Europe.

He is equally an intelligent guide to broader geo-political trends in a number of countries that like Ukraine are on the frontlines of the struggle between democracy and tyranny, between light and darkness.

Scherba has blazed an impressive trail of excellence as a diplomat in Austria, a country with a noble diplomatic tradition, one that includes the towering figures, such as Prince Klemens von Metternich. As a former imperial center, Austria is a crucible for important thinking about complex geopolitics. During his years of service in Vienna, Ambassador Scherba has shown in his commentaries that he can play in this intellectual Premier League.

They are the byproduct of the writer's diplomatic mission in Austria, which has been by an active public presence in the Austrian media, from television to the country's top news periodicals and intellectual journals. He also has been at the center, as well of energetic efforts to promote modern Ukraine's cinema, theatre and music, thus reminding Austrians of the European nature of Ukraine's cultural and intellectual life.

Many of these essays are also part of Ambassador Scherba's effort to borrow from his diplomatic encounter with Central Europe to also speak directly to the Ukrainian people and its elite.

Taken together, this collection of essays demonstrates in intelligent and engaging fashion how central is the fate of Ukraine to the future of Europe, and indeed to the identity of Europe as a community of democratic values.

In reading these lively texts, readers hear the voice of a spirited defender of the liberal values that are now present both within significant portions of the Ukrainian population and within much of its post-Communist elite.

This volume and the high quality of thinking are a tribute to Ambassador Scherba's talents as a writer and thinker. But the volume is also a product of the unique, indeed, remarkable institution: Ukraine's Ministry of Foreign Affairs.

In 1991, when Ukraine won its independence, many of the new state's structures emerged damaged and deformed — including the judicial, police, administrative, media and cultural sectors.

Not so, with the Foreign Ministry, which in large measure had to be created ex nihilo. As such it needed to quickly populate itself not only with cynical Soviet-era diplomats, but with a new generation of foreign policy experts. This generation of new hires, to which Ambassador Scherba belongs, were unencumbered by the ossified traditions and lies of the Soviet era. As a result, the Foreign Ministry quickly developed an internal culture of expertise, excellence, and patriotism, which has sustained it despite the ebbs and flows of Ukraine's post-Soviet political scene.

Like many of his counterparts, Ambassador Scherba benefited from coming to his political adulthood in an independent, nascent Ukrainian democracy — full of promise and challenges. Like many of his counterparts, he also had the advantage of the impressive and rigorous training offered diplomats at the Kyiv's Shevchenko State University Institute of International Relations.

Read these essays and you will understand why Ukraine's Foreign Ministry has been one of the main pillars of the country's independence. Read these essays and you will also be convinced that Ukraine belongs in the European family of nations. Read these essays and you will understand that the Ukrainian state is filled with able, intellectual, insightful, and cultured officials who have emerged in the decades since the USSR's collapse. And read these essays to shine a light on where there has been the darkness of ignorance and disinformation.

ADRIAN KARATNYCKY, the author of several books and editor of numerous collected volumes on the Soviet and post-Soviet space, is the Former President of the U.S.-based, international democracy advocacy organization Freedom House. He is the Senior Fellow at the Atlantic Council of the U.S., where he is co-director and founder of its Ukraine in Europe program.

"I know your deeds,
that you are neither cold nor hot.
I wish you were either
one or the other! …".

Revelations 15:3

"We Will Never Be Slaves!"

Let me introduce myself. I'm a 50-year-old Ukrainian diplomat currently completing my tenure as a Ukrainian ambassador in Austria. My first name — Olexander (Alexander) — is the most popular in the post-Soviet space. My last name — Scherba — has to do with the Orthodox Serbs who fled the Ottoman Empire and found their new home in Ukraine, which was back then a part of "Southern Russia" and "Eastern Poland". My parents were the first ones in the family to finish university. Other than that, my heritage is Ukrainian peasants — for as far back as the eye can see. Maybe that's why I always keep forgetting to water my plants.

Ukraine is the historical crossroads of Europe's East. You'll find all kinds of villages in Ukrainian countryside: Russian, Crimean Tatar, Swedish, Bulgarian, Albanian, Turkish. All mixed together, knit in one big patchwork called Ukraine. It's a country where at every step, you meet people either bilingual (Ukrainian/Russian) or even trilingual (Ukrainian/Russian + a language of a neighboring country, be it Poland, Hungary, or Bulgaria). Ukraine also used to have a large Jewish community, which, unfortunately, grew considerably smaller after the fall of the Soviet Union. What you saw in "Fiddler on the Roof" was Ukraine, not Russia.

Having the world's most fertile land, historically Ukraine had a reputation as Europe's breadbasket. Under the Soviet Union, it was also the Soviet Empire's industrial core and factory floor.

I spent my childhood being a proud Soviet kid, rooting for the cause of freedom in the most distant corners of the world — like socialist Cuba and Vietnam — and feeling sincerely sorry for all the working people around the globe oppressed by the United States. When thinking back, I remember two moments that shaped my perception of the West as a child.

First, at the age of about 7, I saw a documentary on the possible consequences of the nuclear Holocaust American militarists were about to unleash on the world. Burnt bodies, destroyed homes, nuclear winter. After this I was so traumatized, I couldn't eat for a couple of days.

Second, at about 8, I once missed my bedtime and accidentally caught some scenes from a Soviet propaganda film on TV about the rotting, greedy, amoral West. It was filled with random pictures from horror films and wild night clubs, played back to the tune of ABBA's "Money, money". For many years afterward, I started feeling nauseous whenever I heard that song.

Of course, the realization that the American nuclear bomb could hit any minute and destroy our lives was terrifying. Though it never materialized in reality, a radioactive mushroom cloud hung over our heads in children's imaginations. Later on, after the Soviet Union's death, I spent hours talking to my American and European friends, discovering how similar we felt in those years on the different sides of the Berlin Wall.

I am Ukrainian, my country is Ukraine — but at first, I grew up in a reality where it didn't play any significant role. Ukraine was just a "Soviet Socialist Republic", one of many, many ingredients in the big red bowl of borscht called the USSR. We were told, our big Soviet bowl tasted the best in the world. At some point in time, we realized it was a slight overstatement.

The "point in time" was Mikhail Gorbachev's perestroika. It was one of the high points of my youth — discovering freedom. What an exquisite pleasure it was — spending months and even years absorbing all the books, films, music that were prohibited for generations and then poured into our Soviet world like a stream of fresh air. There were weeks during my student youth when I barely slept — watching Andrey Tarkovskiy and Alan Parker films during the day and listening to the Beatles and Bob Marley albums on the radio at night. This intoxicating experience accompanied me my whole life: meeting freedom, tasting it, inhaling it — and never letting go of it.

For those less familiar with Ukraine, here are some more basic facts about her. It's the largest country situated wholly in Europe, with a population of around 43 million people. Ukraine's capital is Kyiv (three million of the population). We dislike the Russian-originated spelling "Kiev" — as it reminds us of our colonial past under the Russian empire. If you reject colonialism — you use the Ukrainian spelling: "Kyiv", "Odesa", "Lviv" ...

Ukraine's early history dates back to the "Kyivan Rus" (or just "Rus"), a large ancient Slavic state that dominated Eastern Europe a century later after the empire of Charlemagne dominated Europe's central and western part. The Kyivan Rus peaked under the great king Yaroslav the Wise (978–1054) — a time when Kyiv was among the most prominent and largest cities in Europe.

Yet relatively soon afterward the usual thing happened: the powerful Slavic state got split by Yaroslav's feuding successors. Historians disagree about what happened in the following centuries, but by all accounts, we didn't have much luck. The common denominator seems to be this. First, the state got plundered, destroyed and burnt to the ground by the Tatar-Mongol "Golden Horde". Second, it got rolled over and divided by the European empires. Third, a big part of today's Ukraine got enslaved for centuries by the Russian tsars.

As to the brutal first half of the 20th century — professor Timothy Snyder dubbed this part of Europe "Bloodlands."[1] Nowhere else on the continent was the death toll as high as here. The two world wars, the Holocaust, the Stalin terror, the 1932–33 artificial hunger (Holodomor) left their bloody footprint in Ukraine, like nowhere else. More Ukrainians died fighting Hitler than Americans, French, and British combined. Including my two great-uncles.

In 1991, with Ukraine's active help, the Soviet Union fell apart. History gave us Ukrainians another chance at statehood.

Today, Ukraine is, first and foremost, a product of her complicated, bloody history. We feel like a part of Europe, but may look like a part of Russia. With our thoughts, we are in the West. With our sins, we are in the East. Most people heading to Ukraine for the first time come back positively impressed, though. Kyiv is a modern European metropole with plenty to see and enjoy. A rich historical heritage, creative restaurants, hip night clubs, but, most importantly, the scent of freedom in the air make Kyiv "the new Berlin". At least we Ukrainians like this Kyiv/Berlin comparison very much indeed.

---

1   https://en.wikipedia.org/wiki/Bloodlands

I'll never forget a scene I witnessed during the European football championship in Ukraine in 2012, when Kyiv crawled with fans from all over Europe. Kyiv's main square—the famous Maidan. Ukrainian street musicians playing Pink Floyd's "We don't need no education; we don't need no thought control". And the whole crowd—Ukrainians, Swedes, English—singing along. Peaceful, full of anticipation, and a bit drunk. For me, this was the moment of truth, with Europe and Ukraine on the same page. I wished it had lasted longer. At some point, it will.

Ukraine has her problems, no question about that. As a nation that for centuries had no state, we have an elite that has no strong sense of state and is occasionally incapable of fulfilling its duties; primarily—the duty to lead. That's one of the reasons we have a reputation of being a "corrupt country"—a reputation that I would not completely agree with, considering that during Ukraine's two revolutions within one decade (2004 and 2014), not a single store was looted or robbed out. That's not exactly what you expect from a "corrupt people". Has anyone heard of such revolutions before?

This shows Ukraine's fundamental paradox and contradiction: we are a country of decent, hard-working people who haven't produced the right elite yet. The elite that we have right now is often clueless and indeed corrupt. A part of it infects Ukraine with its own sins, confuses her and robs her of hope, drags the nation down, instead of leading her forward. This contradiction is among a number of reasons why Ukraine hasn't been able to make a decisive step towards the future so far, i.e., towards United Europe. Not yet.

I wrote some of the chapters of this book while watching the impeachment saga unfolding in the US. A saga that was insulting, to say the least, to most Ukrainians. If someone were playing a drinking game during the hearings and having a vodka shot every time the words "Ukraine" and "corruption" were used in the same sentence, this "someone" would be dead on the first day.

While watching, I had to think about the Netflix film "Winter on fire"—the documentary about the Euromaidan's last days (February 2014)—when around a hundred Ukrainians died under sniper fire at Kyiv's central square. On the 79th minute of the film, there is footage of a protester standing under the bullets and shouting into the camera: "We are not afraid to die for freedom! Freedom is for us, freedom is ours. We will win, and Ukraine will be part of Europe. Ukraine will be part of the free world! We will never be slaves! We will be free people!"

I don't know whether this man survived the Euromaidan or not, but what he said was actually a kind of a pledge of allegiance to the free world, the most natural and sincere I've ever heard. I wish all the people badmouthing "the corrupt Ukrainians" could listen to this man. He is the real Ukraine, the nation that didn't imitate or copy freedom, but re-invented it on her own—in front of the whole world while holding her ground under the bullets.

Our big neighbor to the North does all in his power to make sure things don't change for the better for Ukraine. His big desire is for us to head back under Russia's shadow. Since 2014, Russia has had a considerable chunk of our territory—Crimea and Donbas— occupied. It wields exclusive control over 409 km of Ukraine's border. It conducts a proxy war in Ukraine's East and invests billions in a propaganda war.

Over 14,000 people have died in Donbas and Crimea (no, Crimea annexation wasn't a "bloodless takeover"). Around 1.5 million people have lost their homes. Whenever we had a chance at peace, we saw how little interest Russia had in complying. Later, I'll try to explain how it all started and what it means in the global context.

Ukraine is one of the world's most unknown and, dare I say, undervalued countries—even though there is barely another nation in the world whose change of direction would be so decisive for the global balance of powers. This book is my humble attempt to fill this void.

The Three Goodbyes

As a diplomat, I had the privilege to be with my country at every step of her newest history. I saw my nation grow up — and grew older with her. I chose my line of work in the mid-1990s, rather accidentally. Yet very soon I fell in love with it. "Nothing but children at this ministry", grumbled the first Foreign Minister I worked for — Hennadiy Udovenko. At 24, I was one of the young men and women who entered the diplomatic service when it was evolving from a quasi-independent Ministry of Foreign Affairs of the so-called "Ukrainian Soviet Socialist Republic" into a diplomatic service of a newly independent, free, democratic country. It was like a jump into cold water. From the get-go, we had to meet our more experienced foreign colleagues, prepare talking points, write speeches, and had many other responsibilities usually entrusted to senior diplomats. Yet, as they say, young age is a temporary flaw. We learned on the job, we got more experienced, we shaped and co-created Ukraine's new diplomacy. In many ways, we are Ukraine's diplomacy now.

Whether I chose the job, or the job chose me — I never regretted it for a second. Diplomacy is not only an honorable and noble trade, but also a way to see the world and to meet amazing, remarkable people. On top of that, it just so happened that in the course of my career I was lucky enough to enjoy more freedom than is usually granted to a public servant. I lived my freedom to the fullest and pushed the envelope to the farthest as a columnist for Dzerkalo Tyzhnya (DT), Ukraine's central weekly newspaper. Yes, in Ukraine it is possible to be a "crossbreed": a diplomat and a journalist at the same time. Not very often, but it happens. Some of the chapters in this book are based on my DT articles from 2015 to 2020.

As a diplomat, you get to live many lives. Being posted to a new country, diving into it, getting to know it, and — very often — falling in love with it, is like getting born into a new reality. However, leaving it is a bit like dying. If you are good at this job, you leave a part of your heart in every country where you serve. It's not always easy. Every transition (and the job is full of them) is tough both on you and your family—yet doubly so if you are Ukrainian. Being a Ukrainian diplomat in the last three decades has meant doing a job of constant change amid a time of constant change. They say living in a time of change is a curse. Well, it surely wasn't a picnic, but in the end, it was a privilege, a chance to make a difference with your life.

In 2021, Ukraine celebrates her 30th birthday. The "children" who entered the diplomatic service in the mid-1990s are in their late 40s or early 50s now, myself included. Ukrainian diplomacy (along with the military forces and intelligence service) has grown into one of the key institutions that cement the country's independence. If professor Timothy Snyder is right in stressing the importance of state institutions in defending freedom (and I think he is!), Ukraine's diplomacy has also been instrumental in upholding Ukraine's freedom. At least, it chose freedom and democracy over unfreedom and autocracy every time it had to choose.

In this job, you learn to say goodbye—to countries, friends, habits. However, sometimes, at least for a short time, you have to say goodbye to the job itself. I did it three times. For the first time, very swiftly and dramatically—when I and three colleagues of mine at Ukraine's embassy in Washington, D.C. made a statement of protest and offered our resignation on November 22nd, 2004, the day after the rigged presidential election. Luckily, our resignations turned out not to be necessary. The next day, the Ukrainian nation surprised the world (and itself) by standing up for freedom. The following weeks went into history as "the first Maidan", "the Orange revolution".

My second goodbye was the leave of absence from the ministry in 2009–2010 when I worked as an adviser to then-presidential candidate Arseniy Yatseniuk. As a diplomat, you get a good look at politics from outside. During the 2010 presidential campaign in Ukraine, I got a good look from within. I am grateful to Arseniy Yatseniuk for this chance. It was both educational and sobering. Diplomacy and politics are joined at the hip, and yet their relationship can be strained and filled with pitfalls. Maybe, someday I'll write about it in more detail.

The third goodbye was in February 2014. The Euromaidan was over. Kyiv's streets were awash with blood. Yanukovych and his team — Including the first Vice Prime Minister Sergiy Arbuzov, whose foreign policy adviser I was at that time — fled the country. At the Cabinet of ministers, I did what I was hired to do: promoting the Association Agreement, conducting the dialogue with international financial organizations, and trying to help foreign investors, many of whom were treated extremely poorly by the Yanukovych government. I tried to do my best to serve my country in that position, but at the end of the day I had to face the reality: I was a part of a government that had turned criminal and failed the nation in a truly spectacular way. So, in late February 2014, I was about to leave the public service for good.

My resignation letter was ready when my mobile phone rang and the acting Foreign minister Andrii Deshchytsia offered me my old job back: as ambassador-at-large at the Ministry of Foreign Affairs, in charge of public communications. Once again, the roller coaster of Ukraine's history (and of my career) made an eye-popping curve. I spent the year 2014 communicating with CNN, BBC, Deutsche Welle, and other media outlets, writing articles, information bulletins, and speeches (including president Petro Poroshenko's speech before the United States Congress). And, surprising as it was, by the end of the year I was appointed Ukraine's ambassador to Austria.

The time I spent in Vienna gave me a better understanding both of the West, and my own country — as I could see Ukraine against the backdrop and in the context of European political events (and there were plenty of those in 2015–2020!). The desire to bring Ukraine into this context was my inspiration when writing this book. Partly it is addressed to Ukraine, and partly to the outside world (primarily the EU and the United States). When I write "we", I mostly mean Ukraine. When I write "you", I mostly mean the West. Honest disclaimer: both parts are equally undiplomatic. By "undiplomatic" I mean honest and occasionally unpleasant — to "us" and to "you". Well, I spoke my heart. I tried to explain Ukraine to the West and vice versa — and it only makes sense if you call things by their name. Don't hold it against me, if I paint the future too darkly — we Ukrainians tend to do that sometimes. But also consider what a dark time we live in.

For a whole number of reasons (both personal, and objective), my return to diplomacy during wartime was my moment of truth, my ultimate chance to prove I was worth my salt both as a diplomat and as Ukrainian. Which I honestly, with all my heart, tried to do. It was also, in a way, my chance for a small experiment: to build the embassy as a "miniature Ukraine", a tiny part of my country where the decisions were mostly up to me and where I could therefore make sure that the last word belonged not to personal egos and bureaucracy, but fairness and, most importantly, common sense.

Most decisions that I made as ambassador were based on my conscience and reason, not on the bureaucratic survival instinct. In my official capacity, in all my conversations and interactions, including numerous op-eds, interviews, and activities on social media — I was, in the first place a free man representing a free nation. I know some people found it suspicious, and even unprofessional. Maybe there's some truth in what these people say, although it can't be purely coincidence that most of them are also big friends of Russia. As to me personally — I found it exhilarating to be a diplomat who speaks the truth.

My understanding of the diplomatic profession was shaped by Sir Harold Nicolson's 1939 book "Diplomacy."[2] In particular, it stuck with me that, contrary to the wide-spread misconception, Nicolson put truthfulness and free-thinking among the most important diplomatic virtues. When writing this book, I was trying to be both: free and truthful. You can see it as my personal attempt to reconcile the usual constraints of the diplomatic service (secrecy, discreetness) with a desire and maybe even the duty to say what needs to be said at this decisive time — to my country and my country's partners.

Becoming an ambassador is a dream come true for any diplomat. Yet, it just so happened that the highest point of my life came at the hardest time for my country. Ukraine was bleeding. It still is.

---

2   https://www.amazon.com/Diplomacy-Sir-Harold-George-Nicolson/dp/093
    4742529

And because we live in a time of a weak collective West, in many cases, Ukraine has been carrying this immense burden alone, courageously looking in the face of an enemy that instills the rest of the world with fear. Courage is a rare commodity these days, but not in Ukraine.

Very often when Europe and the world were undergoing a major change in the last three decades, Ukraine had a key role to play. It was the Ukrainian Independence referendum of December 1st, 1991, that put an end to the Soviet Union. It was the Orange revolution of 2004 that showed the European idea as a transformational factor sprouted in the post-Soviet space—and stayed there for good. It was the 2013–2014 Revolution of Dignity that didn't let freedom die in this part of the world.

On the other hand, it was the failure of the Orange revolution in Ukraine that sped up Russia's descent into authoritarianism. It was the failure of Ukrainian reforms that robbed not only Ukraine but almost the entire region of a positive perspective. It was the decisions of Viktor Yanukovych in 2013–2014 that triggered an escalation in the region. Ukraine is the cornerstone. We just don't know exactly of what yet. She sees herself as Europe's eastern flank. On the other hand, Putin & Co. see her as the core of the coming USSR 2.0. On my part, I can't imagine any kind of Ukraine's return under Russia's shadow. Not anymore.

Despite all the democratic strides of the last decades, today is a bad time for mankind. Stephen Hawking, *the* brilliant mind of our time, before passing away in 2018, pegged our era as the most dangerous period in modern history—due to mankind's divide into a relatively tiny cast of "successful" and an overwhelming majority of the "forgotten." [3] Germany's former foreign minister Joschka Fischer predicted the end of the transatlantic West and even the demise of United Europe.[4] The president of the US Council on Foreign Relations Richard N. Haas titled his column "Liberal world order,

---

3   https://www.theguardian.com/commentisfree/2016/dec/01/stephen-hawki ng-dangerous-time-planet-inequality

4   https://www.kiwi-verlag.de/verlag/rights/book/joschka-fischer-der-abstieg -des-westens-9783462052923

RIP!"[5] Too pessimistic? Is it just about "liberal world order" or about "la liberté" as such, the concept of freedom as an inalienable right that has been so fundamental for the West, especially in the second half of the 20th century? It certainly sounds to me as if the worst-case scenario is to be taken seriously now. And many answers about Europe's future depend on what happens to Ukraine.

The collective West of today and especially of tomorrow will be choosing between a reality based on truth — and the intellectual and spiritual blur of the post-truth world, where (to borrow Peter Pomerantsev's fitting description of the world that Vladimir Putin has created in Russia and is trying to sell to the West) "nothing is true and everything is possible."[6] In other words, it will be a choice between a West of values and a West that is valueless. It's still unclear who and what will prevail in the end. But I'm convinced: if it wasn't for the bravery of the ordinary Ukrainians standing up for freedom, if it wasn't for Ukraine's readiness to fight back, the "post-truth" world, the world with zero distinction between good and evil, would have been celebrating a victory a long time ago.

Yes, it's yet another turn of Europe's newest history where Ukraine has a role to play. The role of someone who stands up for what she believes in and who shows that caving in to the enemy isn't necessarily inevitable. In a pragmatic (some might even say, cowardly) world, we fight and bleed for freedom. And who knows, maybe Ukraine's readiness to do that, will eventually remind some people in the "free world" that freedom is worth fighting for.

---

5   https://www.cfr.org/article/liberal-world-order-rip
6   https://www.amazon.com/Nothing-True-Everything-Possible-Surreal/dp/1610396006

For Whom the Bell Tolls

The world had a good run in 1990–2010. Not without setbacks, like the Balkan war or Putin's ascent to power in Russia, with the ensuing bloodbath in Chechnya and the assault on Georgia — but in general, those were the two decades characterized rather by optimism and growth than despair and downturn. The USSR-led "Empire of Evil" ceased to exist. Democracy was on the march. Many Central and Eastern Europeans found freedom, prosperity, and a new geopolitical home in the EU and NATO. The globalized humankind grew richer, lived longer, traveled more, got to know each other better. Even the global financial crisis of 2008 didn't sour the mood in the world.

In 2008, Fareed Zakaria's beautifully written monograph "Post-American World"[7] envisioned the dawn of a new era, where the rise of the West and the rise of the "rest" wouldn't be mutually exclusive anymore. Probably back then, Mr. Zakaria wasn't wrong; this kind of a win-win reality was indeed within reach. If only all of the "rest" had wanted it!

Well, a new era did come. But not the one Fareed Zakaria hoped for.

Vladimir Putin's speech in Munich of 2007 and his invasion of Georgia in 2008 were the writing on the wall, but most people in the West chose to misread it. We know why. On the one hand, the EU was created in the post-World War Two world not to tackle enemies but to find compromises, to balance things out for the sake of a peaceful co-existence. The NATO predicated on the assumption that Russia is a difficult partner of a new kind and not an unsolved problem from the past. The very idea that despite the West's peaceful demeanor and rhetoric, the Russian Federation would eventually switch from Khrushchev-like speeches to Hitler-like annexations was unimaginable in the mid-2000s. It probably didn't occur even to EU's gloomiest eggheads.

---

7   https://en.wikipedia.org/wiki/The_Post-American_World

On the other hand, for the United States, all of a sudden seeing Russia for what it was (a reborn, resurgent, vengeful enemy) amid the 21st century would be tantamount to recognizing that the Cold War wasn't really won by America, but rather put on hold during the Yeltsin rule in the 1990s and restarted under Putin in the 2000s. It would also require recognition that Putin's nationalist resurgence had not been duly treated politically or militarily by the United States (or anybody else, for that matter). Neither Brussels nor Washington were ready to admit their mistakes or rethink their perception of Russia, let alone their perception of history. So, many decision-makers chose to be deaf and blind to the new growing threat. Even Putin's invasion of Georgia in 2008 didn't stop the West from starting yet another reset with Moscow (i.e. forgiving what Moscow did).

"The ex-captive nations", as Edward Lucas has appositely called Ukraine, Moldova, and Georgia,[8] were less enthused than others in these two decades. And this for two reasons. First, in the era of global growth, their people remained poor. Second, in the age of other Eastern and Central Europeans moving towards the EU and NATO, the future of these countries remained unclear. The EU failed to provide them with even the vaguest roadmap towards membership (although even a mere informal "Once you will be ready, you will be in" pat on a shoulder would have sufficed), and NATO didn't dare accept them. They were left back in EU's and America's blind spot—while Putin's resurgent Russia kept pressing on. So, it was your classic "between the rock and a hard place" kind of a situation.

The in-between countries seemed like a possible battlefield—not because the West saw this region as its part of the global pie and was willing to fight for it, but rather because dropping this part of the pie altogether would have been too messy and too humiliating. And yet it *was* "dropped". And it got messy. And it got humiliating—at first in Syria, where the EU and NATO were remarkably absent and where the United States was actively confronted by the Russian Federation but chose not to push back. And then Ukraine

---

8   https://cepa.org/wrong-map/

got attacked and was left bleeding—for sticking up for the West and undermining Putin's chances of rebuilding a USSR 2.0.

When addressing the US Congress in September 2014, Ukraine's President Petro Poroshenko asked America to supply Ukraine's army with lethal weapons to push back against Russian aggression. He uttered the words that went viral in political Washington: Ukrainian soldiers "need more military equipment—both non-lethal and lethal. Blankets and night-vision goggles are important, but one cannot win a war with blankets". The State Department wasn't happy. Poroshenko wasn't supposed to ask for lethal weapons—and yet, he did. He did what a president does: he said what was on his citizens' minds. But on the minds of the State Department apparently was: let's not anger Russia!

I know this because I wrote that speech—and was almost certain that "the blanket" part would be left out (working outside of Poroshenko's presidential administration, I couldn't follow up and be sure what would happen with the text). I was criticized later for that line. Frankly, I still don't know why it didn't get kiboshed and why the speech was read almost exactly as I wrote it. But an even bigger mystery to me is this: how could a mere mentioning of giving Ukraine—America's key partner in the region—a weapon to defend herself in a truly existential fight, cause this kind of reaction?

Ukraine and Syria weren't just "a canary in the coal mine". The two nations chose freedom over despotism and both were punished for it. One was bombed out; the other is being destroyed in a more sophisticated way. In the meantime, nothing has changed: the "free world" wants to be partners with the side who destroys freedom. How is this even possible?

The Trump presidency hasn't been a good time for Ukraine-US relations, largely due to Mr. Trump's personal animosity towards Ukraine and apparent affinity with Russia. Ukraine doesn't have a problem with Donald Trump and even less with the Republican party—it was the US president who seemed to personally have a problem with Ukraine. But again, it all started before the 45th president got elected. In 2014, when asked by Thomas Friedman of the New York Times, what happens if President Vladimir Putin rolls his troops into Ukraine, Barack Obama responded that in that case, there would be new sanctions and that "trying to find our way back to a cooperative functioning relationship with Russia during the remainder of my term … [would] be much more difficult."⁹ This cold, passionless response amid August 2014, the bloodiest month of Russia's war on Ukraine's freedom, left many Ukrainians speechless.

With all due respect, I think that if America wants to be seen as a leader of the West, if it is worried about the "cooperative functioning relationship" not only with murdering dictators, but also with the freedom-loving countries who get harassed by those dictators; if the very term "free world" isn't to end up in the dustbin of history — then the United States and the West more generally can't afford to be so vague in drawing the line between good and evil. Even more so, they certainly can't afford to draw no line at all, as happened during the infamous Putin/Trump press conference in Helsinki, 2018.

In Georgia, Ukraine and Syria, Putin declared a global war on freedom. A war that the West chose not to see in its true dimension because it wasn't the West who was bleeding. After Ukraine, it was the turn of Belarus. Hundreds of thousands got beaten, suppressed, and harassed in Minsk and other Belarusian cities, with Russia's clear backing. Meanwhile, "the free world" was almost openly looking for a compromise with Moscow over the destiny of this sovereign nation. Remember the numerous tweets and articles discussing whether "the Armenian model" (a full and official refusal to pursue the EU- and NATO-membership in exchange for Russia's support) would be the right "deal" for Belarus? Ironically, right after this, the Armenian-Azerbaijani war flamed up.

Time and again, the West tries to find something that doesn't exist: a compromise between freedom and unfreedom. The sad irony is: Moscow doesn't bother to give the West even an appearance of a "deal". Time and again, it sends the West a clear message: in the post-Soviet space, in "Russia's backyard" — and at any place in the world that it proclaims its "zone of interest" — Moscow

---

9   https://www.nytimes.com/2014/08/09/opinion/president-obama-thomas-l-friedman-iraq-and-world-affairs.html

doesn't compromise. It wants it all, and it wants it now — while the West can discuss "mutual face-saving options", "diplomatic solutions", "multilateral negotiation formats" till it's blue in the face — and make a reset after a reset after a reset. Reset is what politicians do when they don't know what to do. Or if they don't have the guts to do the right thing.

Georgia, Syria, Ukraine, Belarus ... — the list will inevitably grow with years, as the world's nations won't stop choosing freedom over unfreedom. At some point, Russia might be on the list too. How long is the "free world" planning to look away, as the Russian leadership, these empty-eyed ex-KGB operatives, will cement despotism wherever their tentacles reach? And their tentacles get longer with every year.

Vladimir Putin has created a kind of an around-the-clock global repair service for broken dictatorships: the number one go-to destination for failing authoritarian leaders the world over. So far, it does the job, with thousands of people dead, with new democracies bleeding, and with the West either passively watching or eagerly co-financing this political enterprise via joint ventures like the Nordstream-2 pipeline.

At some point, the US and EU will have to face the bitter truth: Russia *chose* to confront the West. It wasn't forced to. It had other options — plenty of those. Yet it chose a covert global face-off instead of a win-win world. It decided on a strategy to undermine the West wherever it can. There is nothing the West can do to change this decision. It can either push back or look away, as Russia pushes on. No number of resets, peaceful speeches, friendly handshakes, and visits to the May 9th Victory Day parade in Moscow will make Putin reconsider his attitude. This for one simple reason: the confrontation mode is the one in which the Kremlin functions best and feels most comfortable, and through which the world makes most sense for today's Russian leadership (for their electorate too, for that matter). All the friendly gestures aimed at assuaging the hostility will only persuade Russia that Putin was right in pegging the West as weak and corruptible.

No, the Soviet Union isn't back. Not yet. Not without Ukraine — and Ukraine, despite all her flaws, isn't budging. Ukraine has the guts to stand her ground. However, in some respect, today's Russia is even more dangerous than the Soviet Union—primarily because it is more capable of getting inside the minds and souls of Western citizens, inside their pocketbooks and notebooks, inside their television and social media.

That's why, by the way, the whole "We need to partner up with Russia to tackle China" argument doesn't hold water. First of all, China is still a closed book for the West, and the West is a closed book for China. If China wants to undermine the West one way or another, it is impeded by the fact that it is so different mentally and historically. And vice versa. Second of all, China has a different sense of time. It can wait—unlike Russia, who sees this moment of the West's weakness as a unique, historic opportunity to go on the offensive. Third of all, for Russia, this is payback time. For China, payback for what? Unlike Russia, China is not beset by an inferiority complex. China is a success—Russia isn't, far from it. More than this, China became successful together with the West and because of the West, not despite it. So, once again—why destroy the world order that made China a success?

Whenever I hear the phrase "Russia isn't the problem, China is!" I know I deal with someone who doesn't know Russia (let alone China). And sometimes—with someone who has a vested interest in appeasing Putin and belittling the danger he represents. Did China bomb Syria and annex Crimea? Did China proclaim and adopt the "Gerasimov Doctrine"? Did China hire and inspire a whole army of "talking heads" in the news outlets and think tanks to undermine western societies? Did China fill social media with trolls posing as Americans, Germans, Brits? Did China finance anti-EU political parties all over the continent?

All the loose strings that the West has—Moscow knows how to pull them. From exploiting the interracial tensions to messing with democratic elections and from cultivating political intolerance to spreading the QAnon crackpot ideas. Provided the right mindset and a lot of money (both of which Putin has), the West has turned out to be a surprisingly easy target. At least, as long as the United States and the European Union put up with things going this way. Victory is an accomplishment—failure is a decision. So, dear

America and Europe, be careful what you decide at this critical juncture of history!

Russia won't stop till it's made to stop. And there is a simple way to reach that goal if one has the guts to do it: make the sanctions as personal as possible. Let the Russian decision-makers, propagandists, oligarchs, and their families spend their vacations on Kamchatka and Chukotka, not in their England castles and Italian villas. Cancel their "golden passports". Go after their money, cut them off from their wealth — via SWIFT, via visa bans, via freezing their bank accounts. Make not only their reputations toxic, but their money too.

That's it. That's all it takes. Start defending yourself — and be bold enough to not be greedy! Russia quickly penetrates your world because it can think like you; it knows how you tick. It wants to live like you and among you, too — without being your friend or even an honest partner. It's a quintessential love/hate relationship. They hate you, but at the same time, you are their "promised land", the place where they want their children to study and to live. Ban the decision-makers personally from the "promised land" — and they will be forced to change their decisions, their whole attitude towards the outside world. On the other hand, embrace them — and they will despise you even more.

Meanwhile, Ukraine (Putin's sweatiest dream and sweetest bonus) is doing what she can on her own — fighting her own demons and the demons of the post-truth world simultaneously. The nation is never full of herself. Yet she is full of surprises. Whenever you think Ukraine is toast, she rises from the ashes. Whenever you think Ukraine is rushing into a new positive future, she finds a new political or moral crisis to stop and argue about. The world thinks of Ukraine as a corrupt nation — and yet, as I pointed out before, during Ukraine's two revolutions, not a single store was looted. With the police off the streets, with Kyiv's posh boutiques, shops, and supermarkets being at the mercy of the protesters in 2004 and 2013–14, not only were they not robbed — by some accounts, the usual burglary rate even decreased in those months.

So, who are we really — the corrupt ones or the idealists who fight for freedom and respect other peoples' private property even when no one is watching? Well, we are both so far. With a large part of Ukraine's political elite living a lie, we have been living a lie, too. But ultimately, Ukraine wants to live in truth. Hence, the two revolutions. Hence, Putin's inability to buy or seduce us. Hence, the lingering hybrid war between Ukraine and the post-truth world embodied by Russia and its eager helpers in the West.

With the right leadership, with the right words and deeds on the part of the elite — Ukraine can turn the corner and enter a better future real fast. We are like a plane chained to the ground by two things: bad governance and corruption (caused by bad governance). Break these chains — and the plane will fly. What we need are reforms to Ukraine's institutions, which nurture the corruption. We need to bring in the ministers and their deputies, the mid-level decision-makers who have the vision, reputation, and the guts to say no to the oligarchs and to the daily seductions of the public service. Once this happens, things will improve drastically and precipitously. Later on, I demonstrate in more detail how this can be done.

We Ukrainians know our sins. No one is more critical of Ukraine than we are. Yet, sometimes we deny our country even the credit she deserves. Sometimes we are blind to how much power and potential we have inside. That is why we are the "surprise nation". We have surprised ourselves and the outside world in the past. And we are not done yet, far from it. I don't only mean the two Maidans that changed the run of history in our region.

Most importantly, Ukraine is the bulwark in Putin's way to reconquering what he deems as rightfully and historically his. If he can't control Ukraine, all his other accomplishments are, if not completely worthless, then at least not as inspirational for future generations as he wants them to be. Without Ukraine, his whole legacy would be questionable. Without Ukraine, his entire organization, this horde of KGB/FSB orcs, war-mongering "girkins" and "borodais,"[10] who stand behind him and look up to him, would question whether the boss got too old and lost his grip.

---

10   Igor Girkin, Alexander Borodai — the Moscow-born founding fathers of "Ukrainian separatism", who were instrumental in the occupation of Crimea and Donbas.

Ukraine and Russia have much in common. That is why the Ukrainian revolution is, to some extent, the Russian revolution too. It's not like bringing a revolution to Russia, and changing it from the ground up must be the West's goal. Far from it. Yet the line in the sand must be drawn: the world must make sure that neither Russia nor anyone else messes with other nations' free will. International law must be respected again. At least, if we want to live in a world that is not 100% hypocritical.

On the other hand, no matter where you draw the line and how high or low you put the new plank of "international rules" in the post-Crimea reality, in every case, Ukraine is the West's indispensable partner in the region, its "Israel" in the post-Soviet space. So, don't look away when Ukraine gets assaulted. Don't buy into Putin's narrative that Ukraine and Russia are the same. They are not.

As Putin has shown in the last two decades, it's not only about how wealthy, successful, and militarily advanced you are in today's world, but also the sheer cunning and audacity of your plans and actions. In his case, it was the audacity of the destruction of the collective West. The destruction was his plan from the moment he entered the Kremlin in 2000. He took his sweet time. Stashing the necessary funds while the oil price was soaring during his first two presidential terms, crushing any dissent, making Russian oligarchs a mere extension of the FSB-controlled government, taking Russian media under full control during the 2000s — and only then coming down to the business of putting the ex-captive nations back into Russia's captivity. The months after the Sochi Olympics were supposed to be a kind of a "D-Day", after which Putin's FSB/KGB would go on the offensive in erecting a USSR 2.0. Ukraine's resistance slowed them down but didn't swart this plan altogether.

If the West wants to stop the Russia-induced decay of the free world, it must summon the courage to stand up for what it believes in. But … what is that exactly?

I can't get rid of the feeling that at some point between the 1990s and the 2010s, the West lost something important: faith. When a Ukrainian soldier fulfills his duty in Donbas and looks death in the eye, he fights for his freedom, and he believes in what he does. When a Russian invader takes him in a crosshair of his sniper rifle — he believes in his mad cocktail of propaganda lies, too. Like the Bible says, "the demons also believe and shudder". But what is it that the West believes in?

In the last five years, I kept telling, writing, tweeting out the story of Albert Pavenko, Ruvim Pavenko, Viktor Bradarskiy, and Volodymyr Velychko — the four Ukrainian evangelicals, sadistically murdered by the militants from "Russian Orthodox Army" in Donbas in 2014 for merely going to a "wrong" church. I rang the bell. I contacted and met with religious leaders. I tagged religious organizations in my tweets and postings. Their public response was: silence.

These four young men, brethren of millions of evangelicals worldwide, were tortured and murdered for their faith. Thousands more were harassed and forced to flee — while the spiritual leaders of the West and their faithful followers ... did what? Looked with admiration at Putin's "conservative values"?

Years have passed since Albert, Ruvim, Viktor, and Volodymyr were kidnapped in front of their families as they were leaving their prayer house after the God Service. On a Sunday. On the Day of the Pentecost. It was the last time their kids and wives saw them. The burnt, tormented bodies of these modern days' Christian martyrs were found in a collective grave when Ukraine liberated Slovyansk. Ever since, more and more churches have been shut in occupied Ukraine. The whole religious groups (like Jehovah Witnesses) were prohibited and outlawed. Where is the outrage? Where is the moral leadership? At a time when the evil has no shortage in leaders, it appears as if the good is utterly leaderless in today's world.

What you fight for is what you believe in. And what you believe in is who you really are. No, it's not about dragging America and the EU into yet another costly war. It's about where your heart is. Where is it?

When freedom is outlawed in Ukraine's occupied parts — it's outlawed in Europe, in your world. As you sit in your comfortable cafes in Washington, Berlin, Paris, and Vienna, your world, the world of freedom is being eroded. One prayer house at a time. One human life at a time. One free mind at a time. Are you sure that eventually, the unfreedom won't knock on your doors physically? I write "physically" because virtually it's already there—as "Russia Today" in your television, as the growing volume of pro-Russia voices in your political discourse, as the hordes of the Russian trolls in your social media, as the hate that slowly, but surely fills your societies. I know you are convinced they will never come for you physically. "They won't dare!". Well, you are probably right at this moment, but who knows what comes next.

"They won't dare!"—that's what we Ukrainians kept telling ourselves till we saw: there is nothing Russia "won't dare" if it sees an ample opportunity. Right now, Putin is busy taking control of Russia's "near abroad", i.e., the post-Soviet neighborhood, which also happens to be EU's neighborhood, too. Once he is done with it, once his "lean, mean annexation machine" is up and running, once the Western societies are split up, weakened and hateful of each other—oh, it will be a different story then.

Barack Obama once said Ernest Hemingway's "For Whom the Bell Tolls" was one of his favorite books. Boy, was it a good time when the president of America actually read books! I hope though that President Obama had enough time to reread the novel. And most importantly—how do we get the collective West, the decision-makers of today, to reread Hemingway's timeless classic? Because, sorry for the pathos, but—"Don't ask for whom the bell tolls—it tolls for you"!

Reconfiguring Europe's Mental Map

When I was starting my tenure in Vienna, the Russia-Ukraine war was one of the burning political topics in Europe – albeit in a conversation that Ukraine was often excluded from. To make things worse, Ukraine tended to be discussed not so much as a country, but rather as a "zone of influence", a "buffer area", a "bone of contention" etc. I was stunned to realize how many people didn't see Ukraine as a part of Europe in the political and cultural senses of this word. Let alone a part of Europe inhabited by the same kind of people wanting the same things in life as the rest of the continent: peace, freedom, prosperity, democracy, justice, respect. It was the demonstrative neglect of these simple human desires by the Yanukovych government in 2013 that resulted in revolution, expulsion of the president, a change of government – and the hybrid war with Russia which has been burning ever since.

Russian propaganda has been doing its best to make sure that's not the way things are seen in the West. RT, Sputnik, and a whole legion of (to borrow a Russian expression) "useful idiots" have been actively spreading the notion of Ukrainians as some kind of easily manipulated people, ready to take to the streets and fight to the death, just because their "puppet masters" in America wanted it that way. In short, an odd crowd doing things that are unfathomable to most Europeans. And yes, many consumers of propaganda in the West have happily lapped up this line.

Russian propaganda sold a lie to cover the truth. And the truth was that Ukraine's revolution was nothing else but the continuation of the events that created the Europe of today in the late 1980s and early 1990s. Ukraine breaking free from Russia's shadow was United Europe reaching beyond the line that separated the conventional and unconventional vision of the future of the EU. It was too unexpected, too puzzling for many Europeans. Traditionally, they imagined the EU within Poland's border to Ukraine. Not too many were capable of recognizing the simple fact that ideas sometimes tend to have a life of their own – and yes, sometimes they sprout unexpectedly through the thick layers of bad history, bad luck, and bad karma, like the European idea sprouted in 2004 and 2013–2014 in Ukraine — changing the run of history in a whole region. Maybe, even beyond.

To quote from a recent Edward Lucas article:

> The idea of a prosperous, civilized western Europe contrasting with a barbaric and backward east was always insulting and ahistorical. But since 1989 it has become wholly out-of-date. One of the great achievements of the three decades since communism collapsed is that Europeans of all kinds have reconfigured their mental maps. For the ex-captive nations, London, Berlin, and Paris now seem a lot closer than Moscow. How long a country was under communist rule, and what it experienced, is like asking what happened during the Hundred Years War: interesting for historians, but largely irrelevant for the present day.[11]

Ukrainians are among the Europeans whose mental maps have been reconfigured fundamentally since as early as the 1990s. At the same time, many people in central Europe have experienced no change at all to their mental maps — for the simple reason that their personal reality stayed largely the same during Europe's great turn of 1989–1990. They lived in freedom and prosperity before and they had even more freedom and prosperity after. The farther to the West from the so-called "Socialist block" and the "post-Soviet space", the more conserved is this perception of the "European neighborhood".

But even close to Ukraine's borders it's not much different. If I only had a nickel for every time someone told me in Vienna "Mister Ambassador, geographically Ukraine is closer to us than Switzerland, but it feels like so far away!". Well, I understood what they meant. And it was largely a part of my job to change this state of affairs. Writing this book is supposed to serve this goal, too.

Of course, if the idea of freedom isn't strange to you, Ukraine shouldn't be that far away from your world. After all, it was Ukraine who in 2013–2014 paid a higher price for freedom than any European nation in modern history. It's still paying it, while many people who live in freedom and take it for granted prefer to look away. As an ambassador, I wanted to bring Ukrainian events into

---

11   https://www.cepa.org/wrong-map

the context of Europe's newest history, to make Ukraine's sacrifice and dedication more visible for average Europeans.

Think of the fall of the Berlin wall, when Eastern Germans got sick and tired of living behind the barbed wire and daydreaming about joining the West. Think of the Velvet Revolution in Czechoslovakia, where the nation led by dissidents and intelligentsia, with immense support in Europe, forced their government to open up the borders and resign peacefully. Doesn't it remind you of the Orange Revolution of 2004 and the first two relatively peaceful months of the Euromaidan 2013–2014, before it turned violent? And didn't the pictures of the 1989 revolution in Romania come to mind when looking at the bloody culmination of the Euromaidan in February 2014? Naturally, with the key difference that our Ukrainian "Ceausescu" was allowed to leave, and our "Securitate" wasn't massacred as happened in Romania in 1989.

Of course, drawing historic parallels is a risky business. There are similarities and there are differences. On top of that, there are similarities real and there are similarities imagined. Yet, no matter how you approach the subject, clearly and undoubtedly the most striking difference between now and then is that the decision-maker in the Kremlin today is very different from the one who was calling the shots in 1989 and 1990. Unlike Mikhail Gorbachev in the late 1980s, Vladimir Putin sees the expansion of the European idea as an infringement on the part of the world that, in his understanding, falls under Russia's "jurisdiction".

Putin has no scruples whatsoever in stopping it. Billions of dollars of economic loss, thousands of dead, millions of refugees, the destroyed perspectives of the Russian economy (let alone the economic pains of Russia's partners in Europe because of the sanctions!) – he stops at nothing to make sure that Europe and democracy don't expand further into the East. Putin and a considerable number of Russians seem to be still convinced that "Ukrainians and Russians are basically the same people", and therefore Russia has a legitimate right to control this space.

No, we are not the same people. And no one has the right to infringe on Ukraine's sovereignty. Sadly, the more Putin & Co persist in their misconception, the more they destroy all things positive that indeed once connected these two nations. However, Vladimir Putin and his KGB pals are okay with destroying things. It's what they do professionally.

Russia wants the world to believe that the Ukrainian revolution was not a revolution, that the war is not the war, and that Europe has nothing to do with it. Billions of dollars were invested to fool and mislead the world. As stated before, surprisingly, very often it works. People get fooled because they want to get fooled — and because the post-2014 reality in Europe is so much scarier and so much harder to deal with than the lies of the Russian propaganda. After all, there are so many legitimate reasons to believe a lie: greed, arrogance, exhaustion, egoism, confusion, stupidity, obtuseness ... And there is only one reason not to: because it's a lie.

Words matter, especially amid Russia's propaganda onslaught on the West. After decades of relative peace in Europe, people (understandably!) are extremely uncomfortable with letting the very word "war" back into their lives. Luckily, there are so many euphemisms to circumvent it. For instance, there is a whole menu of descriptions of Russia's covert war on Ukraine: "the Ukraine crisis", "the tensions in and around Ukraine", "the ongoing bloodshed on Europe's eastern border" etc. I once heard a political scientist (surely with tongue at least partly in cheek) use the term "the current lack of understanding between Russia and Ukraine". In early 2016, I heard a university professor talk (in all earnestness!) about "tensions that can spill over into a full-blown war if Americans supply Ukraine with lethal weapons". Apparently, by the measures of this professor, the lethal weapons in the hands of Russian soldiers and mercenaries were okay, and thousands of dead and hundreds of thousands on the run didn't really qualify as a "full-blown war".

The Euromaidan and Russia's ensuing covert war on Ukraine are the two intertwined, co-dependent events of the 21st century that can't be understood one without another. More than this, I think the whole last decade in this region can't be really understood without a sober look at the events of 2013, the year that can be rightly seen as the watershed in the history of the post-Soviet space.

Euromaidan. Flashback

By 2013, the majority of Ukrainians were tired of Ukraine's "in limbo" existence between the EU and Russia. People were expecting a power act, an overdue decision to move one way or another. And because the Yanukovych government, like all Ukrainian governments before it, actually and formally promised to move towards EU (in this particular case, to sign the Association Agreement in Vilnius), a rapprochement with the European Union was what most Ukrainians expected.

It was the 22nd year of Ukraine's independence. In other words, the year when the post-Soviet generation of Ukrainians turned 22. This generation grew up with a notion of their country joining in with United Europe at some point. All the enlargement waves of the EU, all the celebration of Europe "finally becoming one" didn't go unnoticed in the rest of the continent. And this might come as a surprise to some, but Ukraine always took the word "finally" with a grain of salt. There were three things that the pro-Western politically active part of Ukrainian society broadly agreed upon. First, like the Baltic nations and other EU newcomers before us, we too had a chance of integrating with Europe. Second, we blew it, because we weren't good enough and didn't do the "homework". Third, nevertheless, we were on the way, and eventually, our day would come.

The Vilnius summit on November 29th, 2013, became, in the eyes of many Ukrainians, the day of their country firmly moving in the same direction as other East Europeans before us. The disappointment of the days when Europe celebrated its reunification and we felt like we had been left out in the rain, the political promises given and broken over decades, the whole bizarro world of the Yanukovych presidency — it all came down to this one point in space and time and to one question: will or won't he sign? We know what happened next. What was anticipated as the moment of truth became the moment of deception and treason. Nothing was signed in Vilnius.

In Europe, I often hear that the idea of offering Ukraine an association with the EU was a mistake; that this irritated Russia, overstretched Ukraine, and ultimately led to war. It comes from people, usually stipulating that Europe didn't do enough to reach a compromise with Russia, a compromise between Ukraine's European aspiration and Russia's "legitimate geopolitical concerns" (i.e. Russia's right to see this part of Europe as its backyard). Usually, this is as far as their logic goes — for the simple reason that they have no idea what a compromise between Ukraine integrating with Europe and Ukraine not integrating with Europe would look like. On top of that — as I witnessed myself on multiple occasions — back in 2013, Russia was thinking about anything but a "compromise" with Ukraine or about Ukraine. It wanted Ukraine for itself, one hundred percent. The majority of Ukraine's population had a different idea of their collective future.

Russia's narrative on Ukraine's desire to join in with United Europe was evolving over the years. I remember the statements from mid-2000s that Russia had no problem with Ukraine's EU integration — it was the NATO membership it objected to. Later on, in the time around Putin's Munich speech in 2007, their opposition hardened. Ukraine's European aspirations were not directly objected to but rather mocked as a ridiculous phase, a kind of adolescent rebellion that would eventually pass by. The prevailing attitude was: "We don't care if Ukraine wants to shoot itself in the foot by integrating with those who don't care about Ukraine. Eventually Ukrainians will realize their mistake and crawl back to Mother Russia".

Simultaneously, all kinds of new ideas that were supposed to be tempting for Ukraine were put into circulation — like the idea of the Christian orthodox brotherhood between Ukraine and Russia as some kind of overarching common identity that should outweigh other considerations. Or the idea of restoring a Slavic union, a kind of new Kyivan Rus, in which the leading role would be (supposedly) played by Ukraine, not Russia. Born in Russian PR-labs, this "ground-breaking" concept was supposed to massage Ukraine's ego and to dominate the presidential election in 2010, but it failed miserably to captivate minds and souls. Ukraine's young and politically active were still looking West.

It was almost comical to see one Russia-inspired ideological construct after another fail in Ukraine. Russian spin doctors were astounded: what definitely would have worked in Russia, had no effect whatsoever on Ukrainians. For one simple reason: while Russians wanted their "empire", their "greatness" back, most Ukrainians couldn't care less about it. All they wanted was to build a decent successful democratic European state, in the mold of neighboring Poland and Slovakia. In a way, one could say Russians dreamt bigger, but Ukrainians dreamt better.

On the other hand, Russia scored a huge win in 2010: a deeply corrupt pro-Russian politician Viktor Yanukovych became president. His (and prime minister Mykola Azarov's) ascent to power was seen as a kind of guarantee, that no matter how often the idea of an association with the EU was touted at a political level, in the end, it would be dropped. Ukraine's eventual accession to the Russia-led Customs Union was seen in Moscow as a decided thing, notwithstanding Yanukovych's regular political nods towards the EU. Having his and Azarov's assurances, Moscow was rather relaxed — till August 2013. August and especially September were a kind of a rude awakening for the Kremlin. No matter what behind-the-scenes agreements existed between Yanukovych and Azarov on the one side and Moscow on the other — they didn't seem to work. The perspective of the Association Agreement being signed in Vilnius got more real with every day.

That was the moment when the real pressure kicked in. Russian envoy Sergey Glaziev spent months in Ukraine's oblasts trying to put together a regional opposition to block Ukraine's path to the EU. Putin's Ukraine adviser Vladislav Surkov spread his wings over Kyiv and let his "charm" work on the top floors of the Ukrainian government. Feverishly and unsuccessfully, making big promises and even bigger threats, Moscow was on the last-minute lookout for a backup plan and new political figures in the government who would have Russia's back in case Azarov would flip. The Cabinet of Ministers of Ukraine was overflowing with all kinds of "analytical papers" predicting the worst—Ukrainian economic meltdown and the sale of national resources to the EU—should the Association Agreement be signed.

But most importantly, Moscow was exerting its power of influence over Yanukovych directly. And finally, it worked. The turning point seemed to be the mysterious 6-hour-long eye-to-eye meeting between Yanukovych and Putin in Sochi on October 29th, 2013. I heard people from Yanukovych's close circle saying "the boss" came back a different person from that rendezvous. Well, this must be one of those things Vladimir Putin should have learned in his junior year at the KGB school: using leverage and turning people.

The "turn" became evident to the public on November 21st, 2013. While Viktor Yanukovych was on his official visit in Vienna, prime minister Azarov announced in Kyiv that Ukraine wouldn't be signing the Association Agreement. Comically enough, the news broke during the press conference in Vienna, when Yanukovych was publicly proclaiming Ukraine's dedication to EU integration. As Yanukovych was going on and on about Ukraine's irreversible course towards EU, Austrian president Heinz Fischer, who stood next to him, was passed the note and had to turn to his adviser and to ask: "really?" It was one of those real-life sitcom moments that perhaps would inspire future comedians ...

Viktor Yanukovych has lots of free time to spend in his modest $52 million domicile in a posh Moscow suburb nowadays. I'm sure not a day passes by when he doesn't drift in his thoughts back to the moment when he broke his promise to the Ukrainian people by not signing the Association Agreement. Or to those two months when Ukrainians mostly peacefully protested on Kyiv's Maidan demanding things that weren't so unthinkable or undoable—firing those guilty of police brutality on November 30th, reshuffling the Cabinet and of course, re-considering the decision made in Vilnius.

I was able to witness firsthand, at least partly, what happened in Vilnius. One day before the summit, Yanukovych suddenly decided to reshuffle the Ukrainian delegation traveling there. It was to be led not by his close confidant Andriy Klyuev, the chair of Ukraine's Security and Defense Council, who was in charge of the Ukraine-EU relations, but by the first vice-prime-minister Sergiy Arbuzov, for whom I worked as foreign policy adviser at that moment. The task was: to make ground for Yanukovych's arrival on November 29th and a successful summit. The problem was: no one had a clear understanding what Yanukovych meant by "successful summit".

Caught completely off-guard, Arbuzov was anything but ready (or happy). He belonged to the group in the Cabinet who wanted to sign (along with finance minister Yuriy Kolobov, minister of economy Igor Prasolov and some others), but—of course—the decision wasn't his. The Azarov group was actively against it. Kluyev belonged to neither of the groups; he played his own game. Most probably, he realized where the wind was blowing and refused to fly to Vilnius. He didn't want to be at the center of the scandal that would inevitably explode in the event that Yanukovych wouldn't sign anything. Arbuzov, on the other hand, wasn't in a position to say "no" to the "boss".

In the early morning of November 28th, the delegation was already in Vilnius. One and a half days before Yanukovych's arrival, Arbuzov had four lengthy meetings with Stefan Fule—back then the EU commissioner in charge of the EU enlargement and the neighborhood policy. The general understanding was: we need to sign something. If not the actual Association Agreement,[12] then at least some kind of provisional statement. All the preparation work in Vilnius was focused on elaborating this document, throwing a lifeline to Ukraine's future in Europe.

On the one hand, the statement was supposed to outline a vision for the Association Agreement to be signed at the next EU summit. On the other hand, it was acknowledging Ukraine's "concerns" about losing the Russian market. I.e. envisaging some kind of financial compensation for Ukraine's anticipated losses. By the time Yanukovych arrived, Arbuzov and Fule had this provisional document in their hands. It seemed like a viable solution. Not a perfect one, but better than the embarrassment and the shock of returning to Ukraine completely empty-handed.

---

12 On insistence of Ukraine's EU envoy Kostyantyn Yelisieiev, the Association Agreement was printed out and ready for signing, in Ukrainian and all languages of EU member states. So, despite Yanukovych's announcement that he wasn't ready to sign, everyone was ready, if he changes his mind.

What happened next, I learned a couple of hours later, on the flight back to Ukraine, directly from an enraged Arbuzov. According to him, the EU Commission President Jose Manuel Barroso and the head of EU diplomacy Herman Van Rompuy were close to agreeing to sign the provisional statement, Angela Merkel was hesitating — and the scale was tipped by Dalya Gribauskaite, who said directly to Yanukovych's face that he was playing games and clearly wasn't planning to sign anything. Not now, not ever. After which Yanukovych supposedly said "Well, if you say so, then we won't sign", — turned his back on her and left. That was it.

By the way, intuitively or not, I think Gribauskaite hit the nail on the head and chose the right words: Yanukovych was indeed playing a game. He was a political gambler, a bluffer — believing in his luck. And he gambled with it all — with the EU, with Ukraine, with Putin, with history, with the destiny of millions. He was a walking monument to political recklessness.

Simple as that, in an instant, Ukraine's geopolitical course was arbitrarily changed by 180 degrees. And like a car with a driver reckless enough to roll the steering wheel at full speed — Ukraine tipped over. The fact that, right after Yanukovych's return, the protesters on the Maidan were brutally and demonstratively beaten, confirms that both the non-signing in Vilnius on November 29th and the conscious escalation of events on November 30th were part of a bigger plan. The non-signing brought the violent scenario in motion. A scenario fully backed and encouraged from Moscow.

Yanukovych did nothing of what a responsible politician is supposed to do. He didn't fulfill his promise, didn't face his co-citizens who were shocked by the news. In fact, there wasn't a single political "rake" he didn't step upon in those fateful months. It was the basic "don'ts" that he crossed. First of all, you don't promise something to people, decade after decade, and then, in a moment's notice, take it away. Second of all, you don't ignore mass unrest and let hundreds of thousands freeze month after month at the main square of your capital, waiting for nothing. Third of all, pitting one part of your nation against the other, as he did in the final month of the Euromaidan, isn't just a bad idea, but crime and treason.

When I hear the talk of an "America-orchestrated nationalist putsch" in Ukraine, I ask Europeans to use their imagination and to try this situation on themselves. In particular, the reminiscences of Euromaidan came to my mind (rather surprisingly), when Austria was going through its hardest political crisis of the post-war history.

On Friday, May 17th, 2019, huge news broke — about Austria's vice-chancellor Heinz Christian Strache offering to basically sell out his country to a "niece of a Russian oligarch" during their secretly filmed conversation in Spain. The whole of Austria was watching the now-infamous "Ibiza Video". On the next day, the space in front of the chancellery was filled with people who spontaneously poured out onto the streets to express their protest. Students. Pensioners. Parents with children on their shoulders. Thousands of them. "Orchestrated" by nobody. Them coming to the chancellery and demanding answers was the normal human reaction of people who felt betrayed by their representatives. The air was electrified, filled with anger and anticipation of how the government would react. Not a single soul doubted that reaction would come momentarily. It was a kind of "Austrian Maidan" that lasted ... well, half a day at best.

Within hours, Strache announced his resignation. The president Alexander Van der Bellen took to the podium and apologized to the nation for the deeds and words of "some politicians". Then he said the five words that would go into history: "We are better than this". The next days showed that he meant what he said.

The chancellor Sebastian Kurz had to step down and called an emergency pre-term election. An unpolitical "expert cabinet" was appointed to run things in the country till the new elections — led by Austria's first lady chancellor Brigitte Bierlein; consisting of people with an impeccable reputation and not much of political affiliation. And so, in a short time, the crisis was resolved and even turned into a step forward, something reassuring and positive. Austrians saw: their country was indeed better than what looked like treason or at least like an extremely bad judgment on the part of some government officials. Political leadership was restored.

People trusted their government again. That's what I call responsible governing.

Now, imagine that the opposite would have happened in Vienna, in front of the imperial Hofburg Palais. That the trust and disappointment of the people would be trampled upon. That the discontent (and the protesting crowd) would grow exponentially. That the political leaders would lock themselves up in their ivory castle and, after people wouldn't budge, the police would enter the stage and beat their fellow citizens to a pulp in front of thousands of smartphone cameras.

Multiply it by two months of ensuing government inaction, of ignoring the demands of the people, of pretending they simply didn't exist. Wouldn't a revolution, mass unrest, and a forced change of the government be not only natural but also a human and logical reaction to such a blatant abuse of power? Wouldn't any kind of "outside instigation" be as unnecessary in this kind of situation, as when a parent defends a child or a resident defends his or her home? That's exactly what happened in Ukraine during the Euromaidan: Ukrainians were defending their "home", their reality of freedom, and their dream of becoming one with Europe.

In 2013 and 2014, Yanukovych dug his own political grave. Sadly, it also became a real grave for over a hundred people who died at the Maidan and for thousands who died during the following war.

It's all history now. At first, thousands of Ukrainians took to the streets to defend their European future. Then hundreds of thousands took to the streets to defend those who got beaten up by the police. Then the government came up with a "great" idea to pit one Ukrainians against the others in the form of the so-called "Antimaidan". It drove in by train and bus thousands of people from Eastern Ukraine and Crimea, armed and incited them against the protesters in Kyiv. Later on, many of them became eager helpers of Moscow in its effort to destroy Ukraine's statehood. Basically, as the Euromaidan was taking place, the upcoming war was already in preparation.

Nowadays, many speak about Ukraine as a split nation. Ukraine is indeed one of many, many countries of the world, that are diverse — in terms of culture, religion and language. Yet this diversity has never caused any kind of tension or led to violence within the society. Many years ago, Ukraine's language situation was well described in a "Christian Science Monitor" article about a specifically Ukrainian phenomenon they called "Kyiv conversation" — when one person speaks Ukrainian, the other one responds in Russian, and both are mostly unaware that they speak different languages. Not because the languages are so similar (the difference can be compared to German/Dutch), but because being bilingual got deeper into Ukrainian everyday reality than imaginable to any outside observer. Nobody stood in anyone's way in Ukraine. It was an imperfect and yet functioning, peaceful, at times even rather harmonious union.

Those who observed the civil war in the Balkans, claim that the division was in the air long before the violence broke out. None of that was the case in Ukraine ahead of 2013–2014. It takes a powerful catalyst to turn natural and normal lines of separation into a full-blown split marked by violence, and hatred. In February 2014, Ukraine was invaded by Russia, a country that had neither fully accepted the demise of the Soviet Union nor put up with the notion of Ukraine's independence. This was the catalyst.

Someone told me once that historically in Russia's world perception, Ukraine, with her mild climate, rich soil, catchy folk music, scrumptious food, and handsome people was akin to a paradise. Accordingly, seeing Ukraine drift away was no less traumatic and painful, than being expelled from a paradise. Especially for Russia, a nation that still sees the world as the battlefield of global powers. In 2013–2014, Russia rushed to war for a paradise lost. Incapable of seducing, buying, or convincing Ukraine, Putin decided to push her to the ground, so that she falls, breaks apart, and makes place for the "Russian world". That's what the Russian "special-op" in Crimea and Donbas was about.

Pandora's Box of Evils

The idea of "re-capturing" Crimea circulated in Moscow for quite a while. One of Putin's top proxies on the peninsula, Aleksey Chalyi, blurted out in one of his interviews that Crimea's "return" was contemplated as early as during Ukraine's Orange Revolution in 2004, but "back then we didn't dare". Probably because (despite Moscow's efforts), the 2004 revolution was peaceful and bloodless, thus delivering no pretext for occupying Ukraine's sovereign territory. In 2014, Russia made 100% sure Ukraine's revolution wasn't bloodless.

As early as November 2013, Russia suggested that Kyiv urgently sign documents about building the so-called Kerch bridge, a strategic link between Crimea and Russia circumventing Ukraine. Those in the Yanukovych government who didn't work for Moscow kept wondering why in the name of God would anyone, in midst of the whole Association Agreement saga and the budding Euromaidan, be so preoccupied with a multi-billion-dollar infrastructural project between Ukraine and Russia. Now we know. In anticipation of the coming events, Putin needed a legal pretext for directly connecting Crimea and Russia in the form of an officially signed paper. The illegally built "Crimean Bridge" would have been at least semi-legal if Ukraine signed the papers back then, in late 2013. In other words, it was in the fall of 2013 at the latest that Moscow started making urgent arrangements for Europe's first annexation since Hitler.

The former mayor of Danzig, Hermann Rauschning, wrote in his 1939 book "Hitler speaks,"[13] that in 1934, "der Führer" was convinced that future wars could be won not through military superiority, but the element of surprise and sheer political audacity. In particular, he dreamt of occupying Paris within hours simply by deploying unmarked (or posing as French) military units in the middle of the city, causing havoc, destroying the legal authorities,

---

13   https://archive.org/details/in.ernet.dli.2015.505385, https://www.amazon.com/Hitler-Speaks-Political-Conversations-Adolf/dp/1162934913

and replacing them with collaborators recruited among locals. In February–March 2014, we saw Putin not only repeat Hitler's "Anschluss" in a new time setting but also fulfill Hitler's dream of a new kind of war.

Ukraine and the whole world were watching Putin trample upon bilateral documents and international treaties in which Russia vowed to respect Ukraine's existing borders, from the infamous Budapest memorandum of 1994 to the Ukraine-Russia "Big Treaty" of 1997. "The impossible is always successful. The most unlikely thing is the surest…" — those were Hitler's words from 1934. Step by step, in 2014, Putin followed the 80-year-old script to the letter, while the world just watched.

Russia and its paid "talking heads" from RT often describe the 2014 Crimea Anschluss as "bloodless". Like many things they say, it's a lie. Think of Reshat Ametov, the 39-year-old Crimean Tatar, a father of three, who was the first to shrug off the first days' paralysis and go on a one-person rally against the occupiers. The day was March 3, 2014. The place was the city square in front of the occupied Crimean Cabinet of Ministers in Simferopol.[14]

Reshat stood there for 20 or 30 minutes. Then a group of sturdy men in green detained him in front of smartphone cameras and drove away. Two weeks later, his badly mutilated body was found on the roadside in vicinity of Simferopol. Cause of death: stabbing in the eye (by other accounts, a shot in the eye). You can find photos online. They are graphic, to say the least. Just think of the courage of this man, who stood up alone in the way of a revanchist empire gone mad. Think of his excruciating last days and hours, in captivity of Putin's "polite men". And think of some Western politicians who visit Crimea and lay wreaths to the monument to Reshat's murderers, the invaders (not a single one of whom died during the occupation, by the way).

Dozens of Crimean Tatars and pro-Ukrainian activists simply vanished in those weeks and months. Dozens of thousands had to abandon their homes and become refugees. Thousands of lives were destroyed. Millions of destinies were to be destroyed in the

---

14   https://en.wikipedia.org/wiki/Re%C5%9Fat_Amet

coming years. So much for the "bloodless takeover." So much for the myth of the "polite men in green" who peacefully executed the people's desire to be one with Russia. A Pandora's box of evils was opened.

The pictures of the "happy population" and the 99%+ support at the so-called "referenda" don't make annexations legal. The world knew this back in 1938, just like it knew it in 2014. Putin says, "the Crimean question is closed." Quite obviously, nothing is closed until international law says it's closed. And international law is entirely on Ukraine's side. Of course, all of this was clear to the Kremlin, when in the early February 2014, Putin ordered "the final solution of the Crimean question". The Russian medals "For Return of Crimea" were coined weeks before the "referendum" was held. Kyiv was caught off-guard — and the world just put up with it, as soundlessly as it did during the annexation of Czechoslovakia in 1939.

Russian propagandists claim it was all about the free will of the Crimean population and the possibility for the Russian-speaking population to live as they wanted, to be a part of the "Russian world." Yet another lie. First of all, the free will of any population is the last thing on the mind of dictators. I can hardly imagine Russia playing along if some unmarked military units would pop up on the Russian territory in, say, Siberia and try to conduct a "referendum" among, for instance, Siberia's swiftly growing population of Chinese heritage. Or if a mysterious "people's self-defense groups" with Yankee accent were deployed in Chukotka to ask the locals whether they would prefer American salaries and pensions to Russian ones.

And second of all, in a way, under Ukraine, Crimea already was a kind of a "Russian world" prototype. Probably the only one. It was a peaceful place where Russian-speaking people from all over the post-Soviet space loved to go on vacation. A place where Ukrainians, Russians, Belarussians, and other Russian-speakers could come together and spend their well-deserved free days as they liked. Paradoxically enough, Putin's action in Crimea did away with this tradition and this possibility.

Russia and Ukraine, Europe's largest and second-largest nations, once very close, will never be able to look each other in the eye without thinking of the gut-wrenching, fascist trick Russia pulled when Ukraine, torn and devastated, was at her lowest point. And yes, due to the deserved sanctions, what used to be a quasi "Russian world" is a quasi "Russian ghetto" now. What used to be a peaceful place of vacation is now the world's largest and driest missile-base, with rusty water dripping from the faucet. Does Putin care? Probably not. He still thinks his USSR 2.0 delusion is tangible.

Crimea, Donbas and the USSR 2.0

Before 2014, we Ukrainians thought we were lucky to have dodged a bullet. Ukraine was one of the most peaceful parts of the former Soviet Union, managing to avoid the destiny of the Chechens in 2000 or the Georgians in 2008, whose blood was so richly spilled by Russian troops. Little did we know, Russia was just limbering up with those campaigns, readying itself for the main event. In 2014, the same fate befell Ukraine.

One of Putin's most infamous proxies, the Moscow-born Russian citizen Igor Girkin (Strelkov), speaks a lot nowadays about what he did in 2014. Specifically, how he participated in the Crimean annexation first and then led the Russian special-ops group that drew first blood in the Donbas war (coincidentally or not, this took place on Palm Sunday, one of the most important holidays in the Christian Orthodox calendar).

"I started the war. Without me, it would be nothing", Girkin says proudly at the frequent public events he throws in Russia, at which he is celebrated as a hero. This FSB officer, who—oddly enough—retired just before the beginning of the aggression in Ukraine, tells a narrative about him and his "comrades". At first, they came to Crimea, where they violated international law in every possible way. Including physically forcing the Crimean MPs to come to vote for "independence" from Ukraine. Then, they were deployed in Donbas where they started their reign of terror. Girkin says it openly, loud and clear, in front of running cameras. Does the world watch and listen?

Girkin/Strelkov was this war's "angel of death". But who was powerful enough to give him and another professional military from Russia (on "vacation" or not, "retired" or not) weapons, money, military intel, propaganda support, and political backing? Who gave it a "go"? A purely rhetorical question in a country run by a professional KGB officer and his pals from "the good olden times." The funny thing is: it is these people who call Ukraine a "junta."

On April 14, 2014, Ukraine heard for the first time the voices of two murderers—a "Strelok" (Russian for "shooter") from Ukrainian Slovyansk and an "Alexander" from Moscow. In a conversation intercepted by the Ukrainian secret service and immediately put on YouTube, they sounded almost ecstatic—congratulating one another on a successful ambush of a Ukrainian Secret Service group on Ukrainian territory. They also mentioned a "Konstantin Valerievich", who would be oh so happy to hear this news.

Soon after, Ukraine learned their real names. The "Shooter" was Igor Girkin. "Alexander" was Alexander Borodai, a Kremlin-allied spin doctor with FSB background, who just weeks later became the so-called prime minister of the so-called Donetsk People's Republic. Girkin was at first the commandant (or rather the butcher) of Slovyansk, and then the "Defence Minister" of the so-called "republic." As to "Konstantin Valerievich"—it was none other than Konstantin Malofeev, also Kremlin-affiliated Russian oligarch who paid Girkin's and Borodai's bills.

In the very same conversation, "Alexander" gives the "Shooter" instructions: "Don't you have a deputy who speaks with a Ukrainian accent? Let him give an interview, demand Ukraine's federalization!" Simultaneously, in various towns in Donbas, professional, fully-equipped, and yet unmarked military popped up, arrested, chased away, and killed Ukrainian officials. In other words—it took control of the situation.

In yet another infamous YouTube posting (known in Ukraine as the "porebrik video"), one can see the unmarked green-dressed military storm the administrative building in the Ukrainian city of Kramatorsk on April 12, 2014. A group of locals is seen telling them that Ukrainian authorities are already gone and that the building is under the control of the pro-Russian vigilantes. Yet, the military pushes them away, proceeding with their orders.[15] So much for "Russian-speaking separatists rebelling against the putsch in Kyiv." It wasn't "separatists" but professional military following orders who came to Ukrainian Donbas and occupied a big part of it.

---

15   https://www.youtube.com/watch?v=GdjC1ndlQiU

Girkin, Borodai, Malofeev, all these Moscow-born founding fathers of "Ukrainian separatism" had nothing to do with Ukraine. Given their Russian citizenship, the KGB/FSB background, and proximity to the Kremlin, how anyone can see "Ukrainian separatism" as a real thing — is beyond me. To a great extent, what happened in Donbas and destroyed it — was neither an internal conflict nor a civil war, but Russia's covert attack on Ukraine, an "active measure", a demonstrative punishment for what happened at the Maidan. And historically speaking, thinking back to Hermann Rauschning's memoir — it was the fulfillment of Hitler's 1934 dream of a war based on political audacity, propaganda, and a full, 100% denial of truth.

February, March, April 2014 — those were the hardest months in Ukraine's newest history. The months when Ukraine had to watch helplessly, as Putin's FSB goons were destroying her statehood. It turned out Ukraine had no army that would be combative in a moment's notice. This came as a no surprise, considering that Yanukovych's two ministers of defense and the chief of intelligence service turned out to be Russian citizens. They are all doing well now, spending their days as "businessmen" in Crimea.

In early 2014, Ukraine choked. It wasn't just about the missing military capability, but something else also. Russia went into this war, ready to act. Ukraine didn't. After two decades of Ukraine being portrayed in Russian media as an "American puppet" and traitor — Russia was ready to kill. Ukraine wasn't. The very idea of Ukrainians and Russians clashing in a war at first didn't sit right with most Ukrainians. As for them, Ukraine's advancement towards the West was never about betraying Russia or staying true to it. It was all about becoming a better nation.

February, March, April 2014 … I wish no one would ever experience what Ukrainians went through in those months when they, their relatives and friends were forced to flee and ended up hurt, humiliated, dead; when their homes were robbed by the "new authorities", when their reality was simply taken apart by Putin and his proxies. I'll never forget a YouTube video of a young pro-Ukrainian activist covered in blood, being put on a leash by a pro-Russian mob and forced to go through his hometown barking like a dog. The video quickly disappeared as it violated YouTube rules. I never got a chance to find out what the young man's name was and what happened to him after that.

These were the pictures of the "Russian spring" transmitted almost daily into Ukrainian homes via TV and YouTube. Helplessness, despair, and yes, growing anger — those were the feelings that engulfed the nation. And then came yet another turn in this war — May 2nd, 2014. Odesa.

On the eve of a soccer game, a "march for unity" was planned in Odesa downtown. Participants — pro-Ukrainian soccer fans and hooligans. Angry and bitter. During the march, pro-Russian activists shot at them. Seven people died. The marchers transformed into a raging mob hungry for revenge. They chased the pro-Russian activists to the so-called "Trade Union building", locked them in, and set the building on fire. While some of the fans tried to rescue people from the flames, others celebrated what they were craving: revenge. Thirty-one people choked to death and burnt. Eight people died jumping from windows. In a moment's notice, terrible, heartbreaking pictures of the victims filled the Internet and went around the world.

Despite Kyiv's official attempts at damage control, May 2nd became the day when the dams of hate broke on both sides. The Russian media finally got their "proof" that Ukrainians were not only "American agents" but also bloodthirsty monsters who burnt people alive. After Odesa, Russian philosopher Aleksandr Dugin, one of the devils of this war, made his infamous video claiming that from now on, Ukrainians deserved only one thing: "to be killed, killed and killed."[16] And as for Ukrainians, the taboo was broken, the idea of us killing them wasn't so unfathomable anymore. The wheels of war were set fully in motion — finally on both sides.

Only after Odesa did such open, full-blown hate between Ukraine and Russia become a reality. Only after Odesa did this hybrid war adopt the zeal of a religious crusade on Russia's part. Only after Odesa, did it become so obvious what a crucial role was to be

---

16   https://www.youtube.com/watch?v=dwgn3JGNrUo

played in this war by the propaganda outlets—primarily by television.

The first thing that comes to mind is the now-infamous case of "the crucified boy of Slovyansk." On July 12th and 13th, 2014, Russia's central TV channel broadcast during prime-time an interview with a woman who claimed to have fled from the "atrocities" of the Ukrainian army.[17] Tearing up, and visibly shaken, she told the story of a 3-year-old boy being ceremonially crucified by the Ukrainian military at Slovyansk central square, in front of his mother. The woman gave plenty of details, all of which turned out to be lies—including the name of the square where this gruesome event was supposed to have happened. She had probably never been to Slovyansk before. Yet, it wasn't of importance anymore. The streams of hate broke the dams. Many Ukrainian soldiers were tortured and killed later as payback for "the boy of Slovyansk." "When one lies, one should lie big and stick to it"—whose motto was it—Putin's or Goebbels'?

In May 2014, I was asked by a BBC reporter why Ukraine didn't fight back while Putin was so busy dismantling Ukrainian statehood. By the end of the year, a different question was in order: is there a way to stop all the fighting and killing? Since the crash of the Malaysian airplane MH17 in July 2014, it was also the question facing the West. Like the annexation of Crimea, like the Palm Sunday ambush in Slovyansk, like the Odesa massacre of May 2nd—the shooting down of an international passenger airplane over Donbas was another turning point of the war; the moment when the West had to realize that this wasn't just about these strange Ukrainians and Russians slaughtering each other. And as with all other turning points in this war, it had a distinct, clear Russian footprint. Nowadays, despite all the efforts of Russian propaganda, Moscow's blatant and enthusiastic culpability in the killing of 298 people aboard MH17 becomes more evident by the day. Let's hope this will lead to a just punishment not only for the one who pulled the trigger but also those who financed, armed, and inspired him.

---

17   https://www.youtube.com/watch?v=kgfkWExDrUQ

Skipping ahead to the year 2020 and to the "64-thousand-dollar question": How do we stop all the killing that's going on between Ukraine and Russia? The critical problem is that these two countries want different things. While Ukraine wants peace, Russia wants control over Ukraine. Ergo, the only "deal" desirable for Russia is peace in exchange for control. Or, in other words, peace in exchange for Ukraine's freedom. Russia wants its piece of the global pie back — if not in the form of Ukraine's membership in the Russia-led Customs Union (that ship has sailed), then at least of a Russian-controlled Donbas reintegrated into Ukraine's body. That's why Moscow so adamantly insists on its own interpretation of the Minsk agreements from 2015. And that's why Ukraine has such a hard time selling any interpretation of these agreements to Ukrainian society.

It would have been a different story if, at every stage of this conflict, the West wasn't so obviously eager to reach a deal with Russia, if it wasn't so trembling with desire to be friends with Putin again. Russia reads the West like an open book and exploits its every weakness, while the West suggests one reset after another. Russia conducts a covert war, while the West "gives diplomacy another chance." And then another one. And then another one. Once again: reset is what politicians do when they have no clue what to do. No wonder there are so many of these with Russia. Are there more to come?

Russia wouldn't have stolen Crimea if the West were ready to shut it off from the SWIFT banking network in March 2014. The Donbas war would have been over a long time ago if Russia had stood to lose revenues from the gas trade by its continuance. None of this was the case. Instead, 95% of the Nordstream-2, a pipeline that would cost Ukraine billions of dollars and tie the EU even closer to Russia, has been built right in front of Ukrainian eyes. That's why, despite frequent declarations of solidarity, Ukraine so often feels like it has been left alone, not only in fighting the war but also reaching peace on any acceptable terms.

Russia doesn't want peace. The West wants it but isn't yet ready to toughen up. Its main preoccupation is to avoid yet another "frozen conflict" in the middle of the continent, even at the cost of sacrificing Ukraine's European future. So, reaching peace is up to Ukraine alone. How do you negotiate peace if reaching peace is up to only one party and if the other party is officially only a "mediator"? How do you build a durable peace based on a lie, based on a lie, based on a lie? That's the key question. But not the only one.

Reaching peace isn't just about negotiations (even if what happens regularly in the Trilateral Contact Group in Minsk could be described that way), but also about the time being right. In my opinion, the pain, frustration and despair that have been boiling up in Ukraine's society over years of war mean that an imminent reintegration of Donbas back into Ukraine's body is hardly imaginable.

During my tenure as ambassador in Vienna, I had, for quite a while, a kind of a "pet project": the reunification of the Luhansk philharmonics orchestra. This orchestra, one of Ukraine's prominent classical music performers, got split through war. It was founded by a fantastic Austrian conductor Kurt Schmid in 2003 and got torn apart in 2014. 70% of musicians became refugees and relocated to the neighboring Severodonetsk (under Ukrainian authority). They lost their homes but chose freedom over the occupation. The remaining 30%, on the other hand, either accepted or even supported the occupation and stayed back in Luhansk. All I wanted as ambassador was for these people from two sides of the front, Ukrainians, once colleagues, maybe even friends, to spend one night in Vienna playing together again, as a first step back to normality.

No politics, no strings attached. Just a group of musicians coming together in Vienna and playing Mozart. What could be better, right? — Wrong, as it turned out. "We are the people who lost everything" — after a long pause, one of the orchestra's most respected musicians responded to my idea when I enthusiastically presented it to him. "Because of my former colleagues who welcomed the occupation or silently went along with it, I live for many years in a student dormitory. I am not young anymore. My home is gone. My whole life is gone. How am I supposed to play music with these people?" I had no answer to that question — and ever since, I am hesitant about bringing up the Vienna concert again (although I do hope that eventually, the day will come).

It is one thing to talk peace and wish for it, to speak about reaching out a friendly hand — but quite another to be the one moving back next door to the neighbors who forced you to abandon your home, your life, when the invaders came, and the war started. And it's not only about people being chased away. It's about hundreds and thousands who murdered, kidnapped, tortured on the one side, and who suffered and disappeared forever on the other. I hope to be wrong, but I can't imagine any "reintegration" as long as the graves are still fresh, widows are still young and grief-stricken, and orphans still look out from windows waiting for their fathers to come home from the war.

Have you ever seen an 8-year-old boy who lost his father to war sing his country's anthem and cry? I did. The boy, one of many kids invited for a vacation by the good people of Austria's Lions Club in 2018, stood in front of me holding his little hand to his heart and cried his eyes out. I felt helpless. I will have this feeling and this image forever seared in my heart. Ukraine is a deeply traumatized country. Simply putting two parts of it together and calling it the success of the Minsk process won't work. Maybe it's what Russia wants, but it's definitely not in the interest of Ukraine — or stable peace for that matter, either.

The war needs to stop, no question about that. But jumping to the "reintegration" of Donbas right away might indeed become the explosive device within Ukraine that would destroy the country. Especially since the de-facto occupation of Donbas by the Russian Federation got quite de-jure when Russian passports were handed out to thousands of Ukrainian citizens in the occupied territories in 2019. Those passports won't be voided or claimed back by Russia, will they?

"Jumping in" is the last thing needed in this war. The tactic of small steps is the only way ahead. For starters, what about stopping the Russian hate factory on the TV and online that has been running 24/7 for at least the last two decades? Stop picturing modern Ukrainians as (to quote Aleksandr Dugin's VKontakte account) "the race of degenerates who crawled up from the sewage". And yes — it can be quickly done in a country where one person controls all media! Stop producing hate and lies on a conveyer belt — and the stream of bloodshed will dry out. It will be economic logic, not military might or political calculation, that will bring Donbas (and Crimea) back to Ukraine. But this won't happen before the minds and souls cool down.

Russia spent six years convincing itself and the world that Ukrainians were bloodthirsty murderers, so that the de-facto occupation of Ukrainian territory would seem like a way of defending the locals. And yes, there have been atrocities on both sides. Only it wasn't Ukrainian citizens with Ukrainian weapons and Ukrainian flags that came to Russia, but the other way around. It wasn't Ukraine who started this war, but the other way around.

Let me once again name the names: Reshat Ametov, a civilian pro-Ukrainian Crimean Tatar, the first victim in Crimea. Detained (or rather kidnapped) on March 3rd, 2014. Tortured, murdered by Putin's "polite men", found by the roadside near Simferopol on March 15th (symbolically, on the eve of the so-called "referendum"); Gennadiy Bilichenko, a Ukrainian SBU officer, was the first victim in Donbas. Murdered by the Russian officer Igor Girkin during the ambush in Slovyansk on April 13th, 2014.

Half a year before this happened, in the early fall of 2013, I was invited for a lunch by a high-ranking Russian diplomat in Kyiv, the deputy chief of mission at that point (one of my duties back then was to keep in touch with foreign diplomats accredited in Kyiv). We set at a restaurant sharing Ukrainian food and some Russian vodka. We were almost done with the entrée when he all of a sudden very earnestly said: "Olexander, big things will happen in Russia after the Sochi Olympics of 2014". Then, he painted a picture that gave me the goosebumps.

Apparently, according to the grand plan of some people in Moscow, the Sochi Olympics of 2014 were supposed to be some kind of historical turning point. After this, all the liberal forces in Russia would be crushed, and Putin would get down to the business of swiftly putting together some kind of a Soviet Union 2.0. Returning Ukraine to "Mother Russia" was the key part of that plan. He warned me that it would be "a difficult time for Ukraine" and that I will have to choose between my "pro-Western illusions" and the new Russia-controlled reality that was about to descend on the region.

It wasn't an attempt to "turn" me. It wasn't even a threat. This diplomat spoke with a quiet voice as if it was a decided thing—not only that Russia would turn much darker in the coming years, but also that this darkness would engulf this part of the continent in its entirety. However, what was darkness to me was something different to him. Namely, he saw it as the restoration of a natural order, of the division of the world into America- and Russia-controlled parts, a return to a time when it all made sense. For a second, I even had this strange thought—what if this whole terrifying plan that would inevitably cost thousands of lives was nothing but these old men's weird, nostalgic fantasy of returning to the era of their youth? Theirs and Putin's.

I often recalled this conversation after the Sochi Olympics. Probably, the "grand plan" was initially bigger than just Crimea getting chopped off and Russian special-ops groups being deployed in Donbas. The most important goal wasn't reached: Ukraine didn't crawl back to Russia. The remaining Russian liberals weren't "kicked out", as my fellow diplomat predicted. Yet also they didn't stand in Putin's way when he broke all possible rules in Crimea and antagonized the world, just to get at least something out of his lost game in Ukraine.

Two years after the Maidan, this Russian diplomat traveled home for a vacation and died of a stroke, like a whole number of top Russian diplomats did in those years. I strongly suspect that, like many "number twos" in the Russian embassies throughout the world, he was with FSB (the KGB's successor). Often, it's they (and not the ambassador) who are really in charge. And yes, I know that he meant what he said when talking about the "after Sochi" plan. I also think that this plan has been (with some significant corrections, of course) in progress ever since.

Putin is in war mode—not only with Ukraine but the West in general. Elections get attacked. Politicians get bought. Borders get redrawn. Territories get annexed. Russian propaganda TV is in every Western home, featuring stars as seasoned and mainstream as Larry King. Yet, because it's mostly Ukrainians and Syrians who get killed, the collective West chooses to be oblivious about the very scope of Putin's endeavor.

Make no mistake: Putin won't stop in Ukraine. His ambition of re-creating a new kind of USSR means building a global power similar to the Soviet Union, but more capable, adaptable, malicious. An upgrade. Russia wants to feel like the neo-Soviet empire of the new era. Once it has Ukraine — it will start to act like one, even on a larger scale than it does now. And the threat to the world will be even worse than in the Soviet era, because the world is weaker. These aren't the 1980's. Ronald Reagan and Margaret Thatcher are long gone. The mood is different. Is the West ready to face this new Russia? Does it even want to be ready?

RT, Sputnik, troll factories, spin doctors, "useful idiots", hackers — their name is legion. It's a plague that befalls modern societies. By now, we know enough to recognize its symptoms. First: the nation starts doubting itself and the basic truths, about democracy, freedom, solidarity. Second: the nation loses the distinction between good and evil. Third: the division and distrust in government start dominating the political discourse. Result: the institutions are weakened; the nation is split and unready to defend itself.

This is the threat. What is the remedy? Alertness, unity, smart personal sanctions against the one who actively injects western societies with this virus. The more personal, the better. "United we stand — divided we fall" — for the West, this warning is more valid than at any point in recent decades. Ukraine couldn't be fooled or seduced — so it's being attacked physically. With the West, it's the other way around: it can't be attacked physically — so it has to be fooled and seduced. It's high time to realize this threat and to act upon it.

Don't let Putin sell cynicism as the new "pragmatism"! Don't let him install defeatism as the new Realpolitik. Don't look away as he dismantles the last three decades of global democratic strides (and he is at it right now!). Don't let him come to Western homes via TV and social media. Putin is a KGB man of the worst kind, aching to roll back the achievements of the era of Ronald Reagan, Helmut Kohl, and Francois Mitterrand. And yes, he can do it — unless the West wakes up and resists.

"We need Russia as a partner" — I hear these six magic words over and over again. Well, if Russia should be your partner, then at least have the courage to look your partner in the eye! Russia is the biggest Eurasian nation and it has voluntarily adopted expressly anti-European, anti-Western behavior and rhetoric. Whatever is dear to today's Europe (tolerance, human rights, democracy) — your partner takes it with the cynical smirk of an ex-KGB recruiter. If you doubt that — spend a day watching Russian political talk-shows! The level of their contempt and aggression for Ukraine first, for the United States second, and for the European Union third is indescribable.

Take a look at what Russia brought to Ukraine! They didn't just harass, kill, humiliate, and torture anyone who was pro-Ukraine or pro-democracy. They turned the Donetsk "Isolyatsia" factory into a concentration camp, the first one in Europe since the Balkan war. They closed all the churches that didn't fit with the "Russian world" (mostly, evangelical ones). They expelled all the African students who were studying in Donetsk and Luhansk. And of course, it goes without saying — they immediately declared homosexuality de-facto illegal. Crimean "prime minister" Aksyonov announced loud and clear that there was "no place for homosexuals in Crimea."[18]

The Russia-occupied part of Ukraine might be the taste of things to come on a grander scale. Russia lays the ground for an alternative Europe, based not only on Soviet nostalgia and "orthodox values" but also on racism, nationalism, xenophobia, and homophobia. And once again, strangely enough, many in the West eat it up with a spoon. Some even carry "I'd rather be a Russian, than Democrat" t-shirts.

What comes next? It depends on how much of Putin's "after Sochi" grand plan is fulfilled. "Congratulations" are due: he has done so much already! A Europe of untouchable borders is gone. Just like the European unity and the trust between East and West. Just like America's "E pluribus Unum". Just like (let's be honest!) the notion of shared values that unite the West. What we are left with is a reshuffled transatlantic and European puzzle that needs

---

18   https://upogau.org/ourview/ourview_2103.html

to be put together anew. Hopefully, not at the cost of Ukraine's freedom.

Of course, not all of this is only Russia's doing. Once again: we live in an hour of Western weakness — and Russia is just exceptionally good at both expediting and exploiting it. It fills the vacuum produced in the souls of Europe and America when transatlantic unity is questioned and when the European idea and American dream ebb away. The West should be worried. Or at least, it should be awake and aware that something wrong is happening. Sadly, this is not always the case.

And one more thing, before we go over to the next chapter: If you do want to be partners with Russia, learn from those who were Russia's partners before you! Ukraine can tell you a story or two.

Ukraine-Russia. What Went Wrong

Ukraine-Russia relations have moved up on the West's priority list in the last decade—for obvious reasons: war, sanctions, the permanent crisis that casts a shadow over the whole region. The relationship is loaded with historical baggage, emotional context, and political innuendo. This sizzling political heat, this raw nerve beneath the headlines, is nothing new for Ukrainians and Russians. Yet it usually gets overlooked in the West. The background is broader and more profound than a couple of historical stereotypes and political clichés traditionally exploited in the Western media when discussing the region, even at the level of "pundits." To be accounted for as a political factor, this phenomenon needs a closer, i.e., more personal, not entirely political look. Here it is, from a Ukrainian diplomat who once was Russia's friend—but isn't anymore. Not after what happened since 2014.

Ukrainians and Russians are two nations whose paths have been running side-by-side for centuries—sometimes relatively smoothly and sometimes roughly, sometimes in a friendly manner and sometimes in an ugly one. But "liberating" Crimea from Ukraine, celebrating it with a mad drunken orgy broadcast on all TV channels, burning Ukrainian passports and trampling upon Ukrainian state symbols—this was too much even by the extreme standards of previous Ukrainian-Russian history. Let alone the destruction, mayhem, and tons of lies unleashed by Russia afterwards in Donbas.

In the wake of the annexation of Crimea and Russia's covert war in Donbas, the two countries are drifting away from each other exceedingly fast and, as appears, irreversibly. Not to forget: we are talking about the two largest nations in Europe. This means a geopolitical shift of tectonic proportions, whose aftershocks will be felt even once the actual Ukraine-Russia war is over (let's hope it happens sooner rather than later).

Many Ukrainians see what is happening as a kind of a catharsis that was long overdue (finally, we are wriggling free from Russia's hook!). Others view it with sorrow. Many think the crisis was inevitable. Others think it could be avoided. I belong to the "others". Before the bell of history tolled in 2014, I believed that with the right amount of goodwill on both sides, an optimal "modus vivendi" with Russia was reachable, problems (no matter how deep) – solvable, differences of opinion – reconcilable, compromises – doable.

Naively, I wrote articles trying to explain to Russia that Ukraine's European path was in no way directed against Moscow and that the propaganda-stirred fears about the Association Agreement were beyond ridiculous. My articles can still be googled on the Dzerkalo Tyzchnya (Zerkalo Nedeli) website. They are a constant reminder for me and others like me: don't waste your time trying to persuade Russia of anything! For Russia, it's not about the validity of arguments, logic, and truth in general, but about something completely unrelated: dominating, winning, expanding.

When writing these articles, I was doing what many in the West (with a various degree of sincerity) are doing now: reaching out a friendly hand, hoping for mutual respect, and a compromise. I was wrong, for one simple reason that I already mentioned before: Russia isn't and was never looking for a compromise in the region it considers its backyard.

In particular, the whole notion of Ukraine's independence was never really accepted as the new reality by the Russian ruling elite (and by many average voters, for that matter, either). Under Putin, Russia wants back what they think is rightly theirs. The mood is – "Finally, we are strong and bold! Finally, we stick it to the world! Finally, we teach our ungrateful neighbors a lesson long overdue!". Ever since the annexation, Russia is euphoric, in a blood rush, immensely dangerous for the region and well beyond it. And the world often chooses to be oblivious about it.

Again, believe it or not, this is not coming from a Russia-hating individual nor a Ukrainian nationalist. I am anything but. In fact, after I was assigned as ambassador to Austria, President Petro Poroshenko was criticized for appointing a "Russophile".

When starting my tenure in Vienna, I had a bizarre encounter with an elderly Austrian who attended one of my public appearances. "Mister Ambassador", – he said approaching me after the event, — "I know what the real problem between Ukraine and Russia is. Ukrainians and Americans want the war with Russia. Americans — because that's the way they are, an expansionist global superpower. Ukrainians — because they are Russia-hating fascists". Stunned, I could only (I'm afraid, rather sheepishly) respond: "Am I a Russia-hating fascist, too?" "Yes, you are," — answered he with the soothing calm of Hannibal Lecter and vanished in the crowd.

I was speechless. The man was gone — and I was still looking for a worthy comeback. Probably I should have told him something about my great-uncles, who would have been not much older than this man now and who gave their lives fighting the Nazis. One — forever 18 years old, in Poland. The other — forever 22, in Austria. Or should I have told him about my ethnic Russian mother-in-law from Russia's Kursk oblast?

Or maybe — just maybe! — I should have asked him plainly: "Hey, do you know Mukha Tsokotukha?" That's a question every Ukrainian and Russian can answer, but probably no one from Austria. "Mukha Tsokotukha" is a poem all Soviet and post-Soviet Ukrainians and Russians learned as children. A "dramatic" story of a well-looking, albeit silly fly ("Mukha") that gets kidnapped by an insidious spider. In the end, she is saved by a noble and courageous mosquito; the spider is beheaded, as the fly and the mosquito head to the altar (in Russian and Ukrainian, it makes more sense, because in these languages, the noun "fly" is female and the nouns "spider" and "mosquito" are masculine).

What I'm trying to say is this: modern Ukrainians have more in common with Russians from childhood than most Russia-apologists could dream of having, even after years of studying the country (if they have studied it at all).

I know a former top diplomat, a passionate Russia-apologist, who thinks she understands the nature of the Ukraine-Russia drama merely because she has read Mikhail Bulgakov. Not in the original, of course, but nevertheless. And probably because Bulgakov profoundly disliked the idea of Ukrainian statehood — she too is suspicious about it. From time to time, she tries to explain to Ukrainians what they misunderstand about their own region — just like that "Hannibal Lecter" tried to explain the nature of the

Ukraine-Russia dilemma to me. She is not the only one in the West with a sense of intellectual entitlement when it comes to the post-Soviet region. And by all means, I don't know how to describe this phenomenon without using these two brutal words: "imperial hubris".

This is what draws many Western politicians to Moscow: money in the first place, imperial hubris in the second, latent admiration for dictatorships in the third. In their heads they are the "masters"; the world is their pie; and they are smart, cultured, and "great" enough to slice it up anew in the 21st century for the rest of us.

Imperial hubris is what connects Russia and Europe — and separates Russia and Ukraine. What connected Ukraine and Russia (before Putin decided to play dirty) was mostly of simple, human, family nature. Maybe one day, someone will even write a dissertation titled "Russian and Ukrainian mothers-in-law in the mixed families as a factor of the Ukrainian-Russian relations." And that's only partly a joke.

Half of the songs in my iCloud (and it's a large one!) are in Russian. I grew up reading Russian books and watching Russian movies. It was probably only about at the age of 15 when I first realized that the notion of Ukrainians and Russians being the same people was baloney. Yet imperial hubris was something I never learned — neither towards Russia nor to anyone else. Neither from my parents nor from my nation. I think this goes for Ukraine in general.

My parents spoke Ukrainian to each other, but Russian to me — because they wanted their son "to have a future" in the Russian-speaking USSR. In the mid-1980s, speaking Ukrainian was considered generally odd in the schools of Ukraine's capital. The town crawled with kids like me, whose parents moved here from the countryside and were doing their best to climb up the social ladder to become "city folk", which included shrugging off "the language of peasants". That's why — when after one of the student rallies for Ukrainian independence in the late 1980s I came home and started speaking to my parents in Ukrainian — it was a shock of a lifetime to them and a moment of unforgettable pride for me. We never talked to each other in Russian after that—and, I think, they never looked at me with the same eyes. This day was a watershed, a part of a new reality, where your country is not the USSR anymore, but Ukraine—and you only "have a future" when you speak your country's language.

One should understand how close the "Ukrainian Soviet Socialist Republic" was to completely losing its "Ukrainianness" in the last decade of the Soviet Union's existence. Had the Soviet Union not fallen apart, had things remained on the same track as they were in the mid-1980s—I'm pretty sure my generation would have been the last one speaking Ukrainian, at least in my native Kyiv.

In other words, just a generation ago, the Ukrainian identity was close to becoming extinct; Ukrainian was about to become a dead language, like Sanskrit. So, please, have some patience and understanding, if only 30 years into her independence, Ukraine isn't ready to grant the Russian language the same rights as Ukrainian—the language that still needs to be preserved and defended. In essence, we don't want the Belarussian scenario, where Belarussian and Russian were put on an equal pedestal—and now, two decades later, the Belarussian language is barely heard on the streets, rarely used by state officials, and has become a rare attribute even at the anti-government protests.

Like many Ukrainians, I am a product of two cultures and two languages. And yet, at least since my revolutionary student youth in the perestroika years, I would never identify myself as Russian or even "partly Russian". This didn't imply any animosity towards Russia on my part. Even now, after all the atrocities so cheerfully and enthusiastically inflicted by Russia on my country—I don't hate the Russian people. I see Russian culture as partly mine, but I would never, never accept the Russian state as a part of me. Putin's mistake all along was in thinking that he could count on Russian-speaking (actually, bilingual) Ukrainians like myself. I'll try to explain here why he pegged us wrong.

Unlike the Russia-admirers in the West, Ukrainians see Russia for what it is and not for what they imagine it to be. They have no illusions—that is why they reject Russia as a model of their future. They look at Russia as in a mirror where they see the sins of their own country, of their own daily life, all the things they want to get rid of. Most of them are rooted in the past. It was a different attitude to these similar sins that made the two nations, related and intertwined, choose different paths and drift apart so swiftly after the "big bang" of 2013–2014.

It all started a bit earlier, though, in the run-up to the "big bang" — when Putin's Russia put on a pedestal what Ukraine loathed with all her soul: the Stalin era. That was the moment when all our innocently murdered ancestors from the Stalin years screamed blue murder in every fiber of our Ukrainian hearts and every ounce of our Ukrainian blood.

The modern time Russians were OK with the historical narrative of Stalin as an "effective manager" who had a couple of forgivable flaws — Ukrainians categorically were not. Russians were OK with the USSR's "greatness" paid for with millions of innocent lives — Ukrainians were not. Russians were ready to build their new post-Yeltsin reality around the notion of the "greatness" that is more important than human dignity — Ukrainians were not. In short, Russians were glad to seek their future in their past — Ukrainians weren't. Each nation made its own fundamental moral choice — and lives with it ever since. Stalin, not Putin, was the watershed that separated us for good. Putin was merely the one who brought this monster back in our lives.

This was the deeply personal and moral Ukraine/Russia split of the Putin era that got overlooked by many — just like the split that was happening for years on a geopolitical level. Ukraine's independence, to some extent accidental at the point of its proclamation in 1991, got more real with every year ever afterwards. A whole generation of Ukrainians grew up with a picture of their country becoming at some point a part of United Europe. This dream, this projection for the future, got into Ukrainian blood. At the same time, Russia chose a different path: going back to its Soviet roots. A whole generation of Russians grew up with a certainty that Europe was decadent, America was the archenemy, democracy was a decoy, and there was only one thing that mattered: military and political force. Keeping the world in fear became, all of a sudden, a good thing. It reminded Russia of the "good old days", gave it pride and self-respect.

Vladimir Putin is a "*silovik*," from the Russian word "*sila*" — force. That's the informal nomenclature for the members of the secret services, military, and interior ministry in Russia. Yet, he is a "*silovik*" not only in the sense of his education and upbringing, but also in the sense of his convictions. Intimidation, not inspiration, is his motto. He is great at destroying and dispiriting the ideas of others. However, he has shown no skill whatsoever in inspiring others with ideas of his own, at least outside Russia. He motivates those who are nostalgic for the past, but has nothing to offer to people who are hopeful and future-oriented.

Putin seems convinced (and, sadly, has managed to convince his compatriots) that the world of politics in general, and each change of government in particular, are nothing more than products of political technologies, mostly conducted from overseas. As if somewhere in the United States, there was a magic button capable of instantly setting thousands of people in motion. Or excitement. Or fear. Russia, according to Putin's narrative, has found the wisdom and strength to disobey this "button" — while Ukraine has not.

Here is how the ideologue of "Eurasianism", Aleksandr Dugin, explained Ukraine's revolution of 2013–2014 in his VKontakte posting from August 2014.

> "They had a country. An unattractive president and elections the coming fall. No one did anything to them. Then Americans came. They [Ukrainians] went mad, started jumping and burning tires. Their snipers shot a hundred of them dead. Then they lost Crimea. Then they lost Donbas. Soon they will lose half of the country. Soon we will move towards Kiev. ... They lost what they had. Whose doing is this? America's. You shouldn't trust the Satan. This goes for the Russian fifth column too. ... I read "Novaya Gazeta" — it's like Satan's black communion. Because America stands behind them. If we don't want to have what happened to Ukrainians, we must destroy America. At least our own, domestic America".

Sadly, it's not just Dugin's paranoia talking. This is how millions of Russians see what happened in their neighboring country — and what happens or might happen in Russia, too.

It's so easy to explain complicated things in life with the magic power of a foreign "button". Ukrainians went to the barricades, not because someone took away their dream and beat them up, but because they are easily manipulated and corrupt, unlike the simple, proud and honest "Russian folk". Ukraine goes to Europe and away from Russia not because Europe looks like the future and Russia looks like the past, but because America magically turned Ukrainians into traitors who would rather wash toilets in the West than start a geopolitical union of their own together with their Russian "brothers".

This is what Russia's leading "opinion-makers" like Dugin, Karaganov, Lukyanov, etc. have in common. This is what unites them with the average Russian. Smart or not so smart, educated or not so educated, prominent or not — "America" is their explanation of everything unexplainable, the filling to all their logical loopholes, the justification of all evil things that Russia does to others, and thinks about the others. But most importantly — it's the Russian explanation of Russia's failure to become a happier nation and more prosperous economy. The sociopath Dugin said it best, with his patented proud simplicity: "Whose doing is that? — America's!"

And no, it's not because Russia somehow misunderstood things or because things weren't explained to it clearly enough, but because the "enemy at the gate" is the cornerstone of its world perception. Russia measures its greatness in the greatness of its enemies. If there is no one at the gate — well, then what happened over the last two decades to Russia's behavior towards its "close abroad" and towards the outside world, in general, was one big psychotic episode, for which today's Russian regime must be brought to trial.

Inconspicuously for the rest of the world, Ukraine and Russia have been drifting apart for decades — mentally, rhetorically, politically. The people who used to read the same books as children, who served together in the army, who watched the same movies and sang the same songs when they got drunk, in the course of years started believing in different things. Their picture of the world grew more distant with every year. Including the fact that we Ukrainians didn't see any imaginary "enemy at the gate". Sadly, we also didn't see the real one. The country to which we felt so close was getting ready to attack Ukraine and annex a part of our land.

This mental difference came to surface for the first time during the Orange revolution of 2004. The Kremlin was building up the momentum and expecting that 2004 would be the year of Ukraine "coming back". Well, as we know, it was anything but. I can imagine the consternation of Russia's high-brow and top-dollar spin doctors (Ukraine was swarming with them during the 2004 election campaign) when they discovered that at the end of the day, for Ukrainians, there were more important things in life than "*sila*". For instance, "*ideya*" (idea). During the Orange Revolution, it was the idea of Ukraine's swift modernization and renovation by European templates, the idea of freedom, democracy, and justice as inalienable rights of every human being. And for Russia ... For Russia, all these ideas were nothing but an America-made "button", a decoy to fool people, control the masses, and undermine Moscow.

Yes, I remember how the Orange revolution ended. And I'm generally far from idealizing Ukraine's transformation within the last decades. Yes, Ukrainian people have generally outgrown their political class. Yes, the rejection of Russia doesn't automatically imply the full embrace of European, Western democratic values on the part of many Ukrainians. Yes, Ukraine has a problem with nationalist and ultra-right movements. Yes, the Ukrainian nation often appears immature and at odds with itself. Yes, sometimes Ukrainians tend to be overly pessimistic and deny their country even the credit she deserves.

And yet, in 2014, in the darkest time, when the existence of their criticized and badmouthed state was in danger, millions of them either went directly to the front or gave their last penny to make sure Ukrainian state would continue to exist. Today's Ukraine is a part of Europe where the words "freedom" and "democracy" are neither taken for granted nor cause for a cynical smirk, as they do in some other parts of the world. Maybe because no other nation in today's Europe has paid a higher price for them. Among other things, this makes Ukraine unique and essential to the continent. Admittedly, in her current condition, Ukraine can be complicated, confusing, difficult to love. Yet, giving up on her would be tantamount to selling out this part of Europe to Moscow.

In turn, Russia is so easy to love—not only because it knows how to buy love. Russian culture is a crown jewel of human civilization. If you haven't read Leo Tolstoy's "War and Peace" (preferably in the original)—you have missed a great deal of beauty in this world. If you haven't heard "Eugen Onegin"—you have missed the most beautiful opera ever written. And if you haven't seen "L'Ofret" by Andrey Tarkovsky, you have missed out on maybe the most important film in human history. In its best manifestations (and there are so many of those!), Russian culture is profoundly humanistic and European (in the sense of being inspired by Europe and giving Europe inspiration in return). The problem is, however: the people running Russia today, "*siloviki*", are anything but humanistic. And they are deeply, adamantly anti-European, anti-Western in their thinking.

A prevalent explanation in the West is that "Russia got provoked". With all the ludicrous excuses that we know from Russian propaganda outlets. "NATO came too close to Russia's border ..." (as if it wasn't the sovereign desire of Europe's new democracies to enter the Alliance because they felt threatened by Moscow, and with good reason). "President Obama called them a regional power ..." (as if they weren't on a confrontation course with the Obama administration from the very beginning). "Russia wasn't embraced by the West when the time was right ..." (the time was never right, because Russia lives in its own world, where a win-win relationship between East and West isn't considered possible). Etcetera. Time and again, I hear the phrase "I disagree with what Putin does, but I understand why he does it". As if "understanding it" wouldn't at least partly imply "agreeing with it".

When in February 2015, during my live TV debate with the Russian Ambassador to Austria, he (unsurprisingly) played the "Russia got provoked" card, I responded with a story. The story was about a young Ukrainian soldier from Dnipropetrovsk (back then, the city's name hadn't yet been shortened to "Dnipro"). A Russian-speaking young man from a Russian-speaking metropole, who volunteered to defend his country from Russia (an unthinkable combination to anyone who doesn't know Ukraine). Soon after he joined the army, his tank was hit by a modern anti-tank missile. Russia had plenty of those—unlike the underequipped and underfinanced Ukrainian army. He couldn't escape and burnt alive. When his mom found out that her only child got killed, she tried to throw herself out of the window. Her family stopped her and pumped her full of sedatives. After which, she very quietly went downstairs to her garage and hanged herself.

"Now, imagine, dear Ambassador,—I told my Russian colleague.—That you would have met this devastated lady on her way downstairs, on this last walk of her life. And you would have explained to her all these reasons you are explaining to us: about NATO going too far; about America denouncing and leaving some treaty, which angered Russia; about Russia not being embraced enough by the West; and about Russia being called the regional power. Would it have stopped her? Would it have meant something to her? Probably not. And not only because nothing means anything to a mother who just lost her child, but also because the 21st century was supposed to be better than this. In the first place, it was supposed to be a more humane and civilized time. A time when human life would come before legitimate geopolitical grievance, even if there were any between Russia and the West."

I still think I was right. Nothing, no geopolitical considerations could excuse invading a peaceful sovereign country, annexing its territory and killing its people. If we accept the logic, "I disagree with it, but understand it",—we mentally land right in the middle of the dark and gloomy 20th century. Which Russia, sadly did—and where it wants to drag Europe with it.

And one more thing. The Bulgarian journalist Christo Grozev hit the nail on the head when he published the following tweet during the political unrest in Belarus in 2020. "*The Russian (actual, not exaggerated) narrative is this: Belarussians, like Ukrainians, are, in fact, Russians, and their national self-identity is fiction. Also, they are peasants, and their culture is incomparably inferior to ours.*"[19]

---

19   https://twitter.com/christogrozev/status/1294926237773836289

This describes both the Russian feeling of proximity to Ukraine (they are one of us!), and hostility (they renounced their "Russianness"!), and the chauvinistic condescension. As the incredibly brilliant Russian actor Oleg Tabakov said in his incredibly insulting 2016 interview: "We have Leo Tolstoy, they have Panas Myrnyi. Ever heard of Panas Myrnyi? We are magnificent; they are miserable."[20] If the revered role-models of Russia think like that — what can be expected from the ordinary people? Sadly, the virus of chauvinism infected the majority of them. Two decades of 24/7 propaganda would do it to anyone.

This was, by the way, the critical thing in Ukrainian Crimea, where no one's rights were hurt, and yet there was one "fundamental" problem: the ethnic Russians had to learn the Ukrainian language at school and to watch Ukrainian-dubbed movies in cinema. This didn't sit right with many. The sentiment was precisely as Christo Grozev refers to: why should the great nation of Leo Tolstoy learn and understand the ridiculous unworthy language of lowly peasants? Putin and his "*siloviki*" were exceptionally good at exploiting this. Chauvinism is intoxicating. You can be someone who didn't accomplish much in life — and nevertheless, carry a "greatness" gene, simply because you are Russian. In extreme case, you can be a homeless alcoholic — and nevertheless be superior to your more successful neighbor, just because he doesn't come from the nation of Leo Tolstoy. No wonder chauvinism sells so well in a greatness-obsessed and yet not very happy country like the Russian Federation.

According to international reports, during the Bucharest NATO summit in 2008, President Vladimir Putin argued, "Ukraine wasn't a real state."[21] Is there a more obvious manifestation of chauvinism than arguing that your neighbor's identity is, in fact, a fantasy? Maybe this is the root of all problems between Ukraine and Russia? You can't learn to deal with someone if, deep in your heart, you believe this someone doesn't exist.

---

20   https://bloknot.ru/v-mire/oleg-tabakov-ukraintsy-ubogie-i-vsegda-by-li-pos le-russkih-262343.html

21   https://www.kommersant.ru/doc/877224

This imperial, revanchist thinking found an equally bold, but a bit more unusual reflection in the religious sphere. When in the summer of 2009, the patriarch of the Russian Orthodox Church Kirill was visiting Ukraine, he called Kyiv "Our orthodox Jerusalem, where our orthodox faith came from."[22] Many Ukrainians were pleased to hear these words—until the war of 2014 put them in a completely different light. If Kyiv is their Jerusalem, aren't Ukrainians their Saracens? And isn't this war, among other things, also a kind of a religious crusade?

This would definitely explain why the Russian orthodox priests were so eager in blessing the occupation of Crimea and Donbas, why the orthodox monasteries agreed to be used as weaponry depots for the occupation in 2014 and why the so-called "Russian Orthodox Army" was so relentless and cruel in burning out any kind of religious diversity in the occupied Ukraine. Isn't it why the Ukrainian state security service, SBU, had to put out an arrest warrant for one of the Orthodox priests, a Russian citizen in Donbas, for his participation in … tortures?[23] A torturing priest—just give it a thought! At times, it appears that Russia is sliding back not to the time of Yuriy Andropov and his KGB, but to the time of Tomás de Torquemada and his Holy Inquisition.

So, as they put it on Facebook, "it's complicated" between Ukraine and Russia. At least it was—before it got really gruesome. Love and hate, proximity and condescension, faith and fanaticism—it was an inflammable mix between Ukraine and Russia all along. For someone like Vladimir Putin, who thinks primarily in terms of geopolitical domination, it was child's play to cause a major explosion between Russians and (as Dugin put it) "the race of degenerates who crawled up from sewage".

Is there a more prominent way to bring fascist rhetoric into the 21st century? Sadly, what befell Russia under Putin's presidency and what attacked Ukraine in 2014 was exactly this: a toxic mix of Dugin-like fascist ideology, religious fanatism, Soviet nostalgia and

22   https://www.vesti.ru/article/2264686
23   https://risu.ua/en/sbu-established-the-identity-of-the-priest-who-tortured-u krainian-prisoners-of-war-in-occupied-territories_n111729

Russia's insatiable craving for "greatness". In the absence of other accomplishments, this craving could be satisfied only by humiliating other nations and grabbing more land from the neighbors.

In the end of the day, there is a point when it doesn't matter anymore whether you speak Russian as your mother tongue, whether you grew up together with Russians and whether half of the iCloud in your smartphone is in Russian. It's the point when Russia comes to your home and takes away your land. It is the point when Reshat Ametov, the Ukrainian version of the iconic "tank man" at Tiananmen Square, stands alone in the way of Putin's "little green men" in Crimea, and they lead him away, torture and stab him in the eye. It's the point when they slit Volodymyr Rybak's (42) stomach and push him into river, just because this local Donbas politician wanted to raise the Ukrainian flag in his hometown of Horlivka. It's the point when they detain a 16-year-old Styopa Chubenko from Kramatorsk, kick all his teeth out, and then execute him with five shots in the head, just for a yellow-blue ribbon on his backpack. I mention only the very first victims of this war, the unarmed civilians — when killing Russians was unthinkable for Ukraine, but Russia, inspired by Aleksandr Dugin and incited by Vladimir Putin, already had no problem with killing Ukrainians.

I am convinced that these two nations initially had a fair shot at some kind of normalcy. We could have had a strained but peaceful relationship of a bigger and a smaller country wanting different things in life, and yet respecting each other. Sadly, we don't have this chance anymore. The martyrs of this war, the thousands of destroyed lives, will be a heavy burden on our relations for decades to come. Just like the pictures of a triumphant Russia "liberating" Crimea from Ukraine in 2014. They are seared in Ukraine's historical memory. And as much as I want peace again, as much as I find this war and hatred between the two nations, who used to be so close, unnatural and even perverse, as much as I love Russian culture — I can't imagine any kind of return to the old normal between us. Especially as long as a part of Ukrainian land — Crimea and Donbas — is under Russian occupation.

I know it's bad to end the chapter on Ukraine-Russia relations like this. International relations can't be just about the past and current grievances; the war can't be endless, the future can't be painted just black, diplomacy can't be without hope. Yet we have to be realistic: restoring at least a part of what was destroyed by Putin between Ukraine and Russia will take generations.

A colleague of mine, Ukraine's Ambassador in Serbia, suggested in 2019, it was time for the world to start jointly thinking about and working on "the disintegration of Russia". In his opinion, Russia was incorrigible in its aggressive behavior towards the outside world.[24] Well, it's the 21st century; a "disintegration" of any sovereign country can't be the plan of the international community. But, like my colleague in Belgrade, I'm pessimistic. My highest hope right now is the strategy of small steps towards peace. That's the best we can do. Defending Ukraine's freedom and stopping the bloodshed – first. Letting time and economy heal the wounds – second. Restoring international law in Crimea and Donbas – third.

If we have learned anything from the last three decades, it's this: "*siloviki*" come and go, but people can't be blind to truth indefinitely. One day, Russia will wake up from the dark intoxicating chauvinist trance that descended upon it and see things for what they are. It will recall that freedom is good, and unfreedom is bad. It will realize that Ukrainians are neither traitors nor "American agents", but regular people who simply want to live their lives as they see best. And that it's OK sometimes to ask for forgiveness. Even for a nation that likes to bask in the notion of its greatness.

---

24   https://censor.net/en/resonance/3149122/the_only_way_to_deal_with_russia?fbclid=IwAR2OB6WzO__Fb5ExvIE9ZA7o4LfQ9_RL6vU-EeNiqsmdB6L-nbwO8Dikjlg

From Dusk Till Dawn

Now, let's take a look at the international scene. As Russia was spreading its tentacles in the occupied part of Ukraine, it pushed forward in other parts of the world, too. Big things were happening in the US, Great Britain, Syria, Venezuela — not without Russia's direct or indirect participation. 2016, with the Brexit vote in the UK and the Trump election in the US, was the moment in history when the world slowly, but consistently started turning from its feet to the head. Or — if you miss the early 1980s! — returning to normal. Humankind collectively approached the line after which objectives that used to be considered essential and even indispensable could be seen as naïve. For instance, the dream of a truly United Europe. Or the notion that democracies should stay together in the face of dictatorships. Or that the 21st century would be different from the 20th. As it turned out — not necessarily so! The world's manual 101 hasn't changed in the last two millennia: *"scio me nihil scire"*. And whenever the reality excites or terrifies you beyond usual — see the manual 101.

Just like the positive historic turn of 1989, the evil turn of 2016 came unanticipated for most people. Except for those who always dreamt that freedom and truth wouldn't stand in the way. Well, their dreams keep coming true so far. No, it's not like "Putin destroyed the West". Yet, perhaps by chance, Putin's hour of utmost impudence coincided with the West's hour of utmost weakness. In 2016, history, zebra-like as it is, opened a big fat black stripe. Liberal globalization was declared dead (prematurely or not — time will tell). The liberal world order, based on the notion that freedom is good and unfreedom is bad, started wobbling. The global project of promoting democracy put up the "closed" sign — either for renovation or for audit. Audit sounds more like it, considering that nowadays, modern western societies get enticed much more easily by the clickety-clack of numbers than by the melody of noble causes.

Democracy and freedom, the ideas that were the driving factor of the last decades, seem to be losing their sweetness. No, they weren't dropped altogether, but they stopped being the banner of

the West. I know people in the West (especially from young generation) who see these values as somewhat hypocritical, introduced
from above and not desired from beneath. Can it be that Western
societies at some point will see democracy as a shallow political
construct, just like my generation saw communism under the
USSR? I hope not. At the same time, it's quite clear already that the
herd mentality and the penchant for simple, twitter-compatible solutions to the world's complicated problems have overcome western voters. Simple solutions and the herd mentality are things we
know all too well from the mid-20th century. And they don't bode
well for mankind.

It turned out that new forms of oriental authoritarianism can
make modern intelligent people content and even (to some extent)
happy. For instance, the unlimited power of a soft-mannered man
with a KGB-background in Russia. As his manners are so exceptionally extra-soft and as he is so successful in manipulating, fool-
ing and even subduing other nations, many Russians are ready to
be patient, even as long as their own nation remains poor. Democracy is difficult and not always effective—unlike the soft-mannered
man, who is well-groomed, wise and likable whenever he appears
on the TV screens. Not only for Russians, but also for left extremists,
neofascists, nationalists and all kinds of "fighters against imperialism" around the world.

Irony aside, it's safe to state now: Russia has borrowed the
Western-born ideology of anti-globalism, groomed it, pumped it up
financially, and brought it to every western home—and even to the
top end of global politics. Of course, anti-globalism, an ideology of
negation of ideology, isn't Marxism. It's as empty as a drum and as
simple as an orange: rolling the global clock 30 years back. Yet,
wasn't that the soft-mannered man's dream, his ultima ratio when
he walked like a duck into the Kremlin back in the year 2000?

Most problems of the collective West are home-made—by the
right as much as by the left. It was strange to see the amazingly
talented film director Michael Moore lament Donald J. Trump's ascent to power. Didn't Moore year after year, film after film, nurture
the anti-systemic mood, laying the ground for an anti-systemic
president? Didn't Hollywood, decade after decade shoot

blockbusters and TV shows with the US government as the world's #1 villain? Didn't all of them together put the whole concept of the "swamp" to be drained (in reality, for the US institutions to be distrusted out of principle) in the heads of many Americans?

The West is in trouble. The world is in trouble. It's scary to see the Putinesque commandment "We'll kill them even in water closets" applied by the world's presidents to political opposition in a rising number of countries. Once again, the hand aches to re-write Professor Fukuyama's "End of History": authoritarianism is on the march; democracy is on retreat. Yet, whenever that urge overcomes you—pinch yourself real hard! A literal end of history is not what professor Fukuyama meant. History is never at the end—just like the good, just like the evil. At midnight, there will be that moment, with four zeroes at the digital clock, when the time will appear to have stopped altogether. Yet be patient: in a minute, it will tick-tock further on.

Remember the days when the project of United Europe appeared to be the passage to the perfect world? Well, there are nations on the European continent who went that passage all the way through. A whole generation grew up in Europe, given in material sense (and in the sense of opportunities) more than any generation who ever lived on this planet. And it's striking for us outsiders to see this generation being not really happy.

It's striking to see EU job centers filled with youngsters looking for employment. It's remarkable to see 52% of young adults live with their parents in the United States.[25] According to a 2017 Gallup survey, only around 20% of the young men in countries like Italy, Spain, and Germany answered "yes" when asked, "would you be ready to go to war to defend your country?". "Doom and gloom" seem to be Europe's new normal. At times, it seems like the EU succeeded where the Soviet Union failed so miserably—at building an ideal society. And after succeeding, it didn't like it all that much.

---

25   https://www.pewresearch.org/fact-tank/2020/09/04/a-majority-of-young-a dults-in-the-u-s-live-with-their-parents-for-the-first-time-since-the-great-depr ession/

Let's take a glance at the transatlantic security — or the lack thereof — in today's world. First and foremost, NATO is about Europe's confidence that America has its back — and vice versa. Needless to say, no one's back is really secure these days. Europe debates behind the scene on what can replace the US nuclear umbrella. The United States, on the other hand, under its 45th president, apparently viewed geopolitics as some globally run business — evidently by the motto "Pay up or burn in a nuclear Holocaust!"

Things appear to be falling apart. And it's not all on President 45. Way ahead of Trump's ascent to power, America had let Assad kill hundreds of thousands of people in Syria and allowed Putin to become the king-maker in the Middle East. Have American decision-makers ever realized that thousands of people who died in Ukraine, and hundreds of thousands killed in Syria went at least partly on account of those who espoused to seek "diplomatic ways of settlement" in these countries, no matter what? If what happened in Syria and Ukraine in the last years was a diplomatic solution, then this particular school of diplomacy must date back to Pontius Pilatus himself.

We Ukrainians must realize and ponder the fact that NATO and EU, the two international structures on which we so confidently and boldly pinned our future, aren't sure about their future themselves. Moreover, our big partner overseas is split and polarized — a political disease that will take a long time to heal. As long as this new American partisanship endures, many sound ideas stand to be cast aside as products of the "elites", and many stupid ideas will be celebrated because they are simple enough to tweet them out. Once again: it's midnight, and there are four zeroes on the clock.

On the other hand, Germany's minister of finance Wolfgang Schäuble is definitely right in saying that the idea and reality of the EU went so deeply into the blood of Europeans that even if it falls apart, they would roll up their sleeves and start working on a new one the very same day. The European project is there to stay, one way or another, but in what form? What started as a European version of Ronal Reagan's "shining city on a hill" might be reduced to a kind of a community center/townhall that would focus on anything but strategic things of global dimension. The EU may very well become a kind of a hedged living community, an island of relative prosperity amid rising global chaos.

Let's be honest: seeing the EU clam up like a shell is not the development on which Ukraine counted when going on barricades for her EU association in 2013–14. Yet, as angry as we at times might be with today's decision-makers in the EU (primarily for their occasional desire to appease Russia), we might miss them in a not so distant future. The coming generation of politicians might be even more "pragmatic". I wouldn't exclude that Europe's coming political rulers will view the world primarily as a business environment, and single countries—as business projects. This project works—and this one not so much. This one brings money—and this one, smeared with blood, is about some small-print, something about freedom and democracy. So, no money to be made here.

Europe and America cooled down and went full "pragmatic". Russia and (somewhat) Asia overheated. From school physics, we know what's likely to happen next: the world might split. Or, rather, get carved up. I wouldn't be surprised if someone in the high political offices or the expert community is already drawing the new division lines. With one significant question mark though: what happens to Ukraine?

Notorious for its unfortunate historical timing, Ukraine got stuck in-between. On the one side, an overheating Russia, who wants to stick it to the world. On the other one, the United Europe project, cooling down and seeking a new balance with Putin. It might appear that a compromise would be in order. Yet what Russia wants is not a compromise over Ukraine, but a triumph over her.

Putin wants to corrupt the EU's soul, but he wants to own both the soul and the body in Ukraine's case. As someone who sincerely believes that "Russians and Ukrainians are the same people", he lives with a notion that Ukraine's revolution is a Russian revolution, too. Without breaking Ukraine's revolution, he won't feel like he "stuck it to them". Let alone that the USSR 2.0, his life cause will remain incomplete.

So, Ukraine must be ready for a lonely existence under tremendous pressure. Fighting for our freedom, we, all of a sudden, find ourselves in the unenviable position of keepers of the Holy Grail. Our only chance is to suck it up and enter this cynical world, without dropping the "Grail" — to become a functioning business environment. Let the Buffets and Zuckerbergs of this word smell the money in Ukraine. Get our act together politically. Curb the bureaucracy. Stop the corruption. Remind Ukraine's law enforcement that the highest form of patriotism is to make sure every invested euro and dollar is sacrosanct and untouchable.

The shortest path to the West's heart is via its money purse these days. As long as Russia hasn't physically attacked "one of them" — other arguments won't really work. But even if it does attack one of them — the sobering won't be as instant and automatic as some of us think. The West's mood reminds me of the name of the Soviet arthouse movie (and a psychiatric term) — "Mournful Unconcern." [26] Yes, Russia redraws borders in Europe ... Yes, Ukrainians pay dearly for putting their faith in EU ... Yes, Putin and Assad kill hundreds of thousands in Syria ... However, what do you want us to do? ... Fighting a war isn't an answer ... Sanctions lead nowhere ... Let's give diplomacy a chance! ... We need to give Putin a face-saving option! ...

Europe's destiny is decided, among other places, in Ukraine, as in Ukraine we'll have the answer to the question whether freedom still is an inalienable human right in today's world. We heard the first part of the answer in Syria. Ukraine will give the second and ultimate (hopefully, a different) one.

Coincidence is as much a part of our global reality as the logic of history. Yet, the fact that some observers date the start of the weakening of democracy back to the years 2005–2006, i.e., to the final whimper of the 2004 Orange Revolution in Ukraine, the time that encouraged Putin to his 2007 Munich manifesto and his 2008 "tour de force" in Georgia, might not be a coincidence.

---

26   https://www.imdb.com/title/tt0124127/

Who knows, maybe like in that iconic Ray Bradbury story,[27] we Ukrainians stepped on some wrong butterfly in our "orange" past—and changed the global chain of events. Something important went off in the worldwide balance of good and evil, freedom and despotism when Ukraine's noble and peaceful accomplishment of 2004 was shortchanged on petty political bickering and yet another talentless government. Now, Ukraine has borrowed a second chance from history. A harder and bloodier one—at a point in time that couldn't be more unfortunate. The West wishes to focus on itself. Russia wishes to absorb us—and thinks it's either now or never.

So, is freedom essential or not? Does the truth exist? What were the last three decades—the moment of truth or a mere mirage? When looking at the West, you have one answer—and a different one when looking at Ukraine. One nation walks the path of pain to the end to defend her freedom. The others start "reaching for a compromise" and offering Russia a "reset" after a "reset" without as much as putting a foot on that path.

Of course, considering the fact that even now, almost half of the Ukrainian population still sees Russia as a brotherly nation, it seems logical to seek a compromise with Moscow. Yet, as I mentioned many times earlier, Moscow doesn't like to think in terms of settlements in the part of the world it sees as its backyard. And what seems like a compromise to the West is mostly, in essence, a capitulation for Ukraine. For one simple reason: a compromise is not something reached at the expense of only one party. Sadly, all Ukraine/Russia settlements that have been discussed behind the scenes so far are about one thing: how much of her territory and freedom must Ukraine yield to be left alone by Russia.

Hopefully, someone is still looking for a more just formula. Godspeed! I only ask myself: has Russia finally realized how deeply it misread Ukraine in the course of its history, or does it still think Ukrainians are the same people as Russians, only more stupid? Stupid enough to want freedom. I'm not ready to give an optimistic answer to this question.

---

27   https://en.wikipedia.org/wiki/A_Sound_of_Thunder

As long as Russia looms aggressive on the one side and the EU isn't really open on the other, Ukraine will be more or less under a siege. And, like any group of people facing a siege, we Ukrainians need to come together and agree on certain things. First of all, realize that we have many friends, but none of them will ever move between our adversary and us. No matter how critical it might get, there won't be any "backup" coming from any side. If the enemy decides to turn Kyiv into Aleppo, there will be nothing and nobody to stop him. And even supposed that Russian bombers leave nothing but a smoking desert across Ukrainian cities—the West's vicious circle will remain the same. First—"we are deeply concerned." Second—"let's give diplomacy a chance." Third—"it's time to open a new chapter." I.e., a new reset. The West will dance this three-step waltz with Russia till a politician of Ronald Reagan or JFK's caliber emerges on the horizon. A politician with guts.

I know it's a terrible thing to write and to think, but it needs sober contemplation. If nevertheless, we Ukrainians decide to stand our ground to the end, we must agree on several things that can't be abided in a besieged nation. Namely: petty bickering and theft, ethnic hatred and nationalistic aggression, whining and schadenfreude.

Ukraine is getting reformed. Slowly, but surely, mister Hyde turns Doctor Jekyll. Yes, we are rightly discontent: it's happening too slowly. However, saying that the change isn't there would be wrong. New rulers, new diplomats, new civil society, new political ideas mark the turn to a new Ukraine. The tremendous mass desire for a change and the immense individual sacrifice to defend Ukraine's freedom moved the country several significant steps forward. Ukraine is one step away from a real breakthrough. What we need is a little more of all things good and a little less of all things bad. A little more domestic peace, justice, optimism and competent government. A little less theft, cynicism, and this Ukrainian tradition to hang at each other's throat at the smallest occasion.

Our destiny is up to us. Maybe not necessarily in form of EU or NATO membership in the foreseeable future (with this regard, too many factors are up in the air). But surviving, succeeding, reforming, finding peace with each other—it's all within our reach.

Yes, the world around us seems to be rolling back to the Andropov and Brezhnev era. Yes, Russia idolizes its "greatness" and is ready to bring ever new sacrifices to this idol. Yes, our soldiers and their families pay a terrible price standing in Russia's way. However, we should finally realize that our soldiers are also paying the price for our sins and our weakness. It's time to bring our own house in order, to get a grip — in what we do, think, and say. Once we make that effort, once we make our Ukrainian house cleaner — we'll see how much stronger we'll become as a nation. And once we do become stronger — we'll endure no matter what the outside world holds ready for us.

Going Against the Flow

Let's zoom in on Europe and the European context, in which Ukraine is trying not only to survive, but also to build a new future. In May of 2017, Ukrainian pop star and ethnic Crimean Tatar Jamala won the Eurovision contest—with a highly political, anti-dictatorship song. In the end, it was a dramatic face-off between a Ukrainian and Russian contestant, a contest brimming with political innuendo. After Jamala won, I had a conversation with an EU journalist who looked like a scared bird: dear Lord, Ukraine beat Russia, in such a dramatic fashion, with such a political song, with Europe's votes—didn't Europe go too far this time in "provoking Russia"? That was the moment when it became especially clear to me: Europe has a courage problem.

Since 2014, a war has ground on in Europe's East. Undeclared, evil, hideous. With Ukrainian flags on the one side and Russian flags (and citizens, and weapons, and money, and military) on the other. Nevertheless, many choose to see it as a domestic conflict. Ukraine's victory in this war isn't what most Europeans have in mind. What we perceive as a battle of good and evil, freedom and unfreedom, democracy and authoritarianism—seems to them too complicated to comprehend. It's more comfortable that way. The lie of the "civil war", a domestic conflict in Ukraine, implies that Europe needs to mediate. The truth, on the other hand, suggests that Europe has to toughen up and change its ways—because a free country in Europe got attacked for refusing to give up her freedom and it is entitled to expect full support from other freedom-loving nations.

The truth puts Europe right in the middle of the war, while the lie puts her above it. The truth is uncomfortable and demanding, while the lie doesn't change much in Europe's perception of itself and its neighborhood. So, why are we Ukrainians so surprised whenever Europe is gladly and even eagerly fooled by Russia?

Many Europeans would have long given up if they were in our shoes. Not only because it's so scary to face off against a nuclear state. And not only because Russia is so obviously enjoying every minute of this face-off. And not only because political Europe sometimes looks like a supermarket, where "Gazprom" walks along the aisle and puts one EU politician/expert after another into the shopping cart. All these factors are essential, but they are only reflections of something bigger: the hour of Europe's weakness.

History is the biggest cheater and the bravest hero at the same time. The heroic Jordano Bruno and the deceitful Giuseppe Cagliostro in one person. It brings the whole generations to the barricades — and then laughs into their faces. On the ruins of the great war, it built United Europe, one of the greatest creations of the human civilization, on par with the eras of Renaissance and Enlightenment — and immediately, during the lifetime of one generation, put it on the brink of an abyss. The continent that just ten years ago was loaded with optimism and reached out to more democracy and freedom, all of a sudden lost its mojo, sagged down like the watch on the famous Salvador Dali painting. Democracy and freedom aren't the talk of the day anymore, replaced with the new slogan: pragmatism. A nice word meaning, in this case, "freedom and democracy — for us; whatever is politically convenient and financially expedient — for you".

No one will speak openly about it, but today's Europe is preoccupied primarily with working out a new balance with Russia — at the least. And at the most — with saving face while circumventing Putin's wars and human rights violations on the way to the enormous Russian market. "We need Russia as a partner" — you'll hear this mantra from all wings and all corners of European political life — conservative and liberal, left-radical and right-populist, intellectual and batshit crazy.

Before the 2013–2014 Revolution of Dignity in Ukraine, the course of history was rather obvious. Two European projects were at the stage of completion: the enlarged "United Europe" and Putin's resurging "Russian World". The extended European Union rounded up on the one side. And on the other one — the Russia-led community of nations, where freedom and democracy aren't seen as the basic human need by default, rather as an exotic luxury. These two parts of Eurasia — the free and unfree one — were about to find a new balance and start a new era that promised enormous enrichment to some, at the cost of cementing others' unfreedom.

The economic perspectives were breathtaking. United Europe would become an integral part of the economic China-Russia-EU chain. A Eurasian railway connecting China with the EU would be built. A "West Europe–West China" highway also. Western companies had already made enormous money at the Sochi Olympics. A whole jungle of financial and other services grew around the Russian, Ukrainian, and other post-Soviet money. Shady, and therefore incredibly lucrative. "The Russian world" was supposed to become Europe's new growth space, whereas Europe was supposed to be the source of new technologies and investments for "the Russian world".

And then ... then the year 2014 arrived – flushing all these plans down the toilet. Ukraine refused to be a part of the Russian world. Russia stopped pretending to be a part of Europe. A crack ran through Europe – thin one at first, but then broader and deeper. Ideals sagged under the pressure of egoistic interests. European confidence in tomorrow drowned in the flow of Syrian, Libyan, Afghan, Iraqi (but not Ukrainian) refugees. The light bulb of history went off. And a new darkness descended on the continent.

Ukraine stood in Russia's way to a renewed imperial status – and in the way of many Europeans to their mind-blowing enrichment. Any questions, why so many in the West chronically "misunderstand" us Ukrainians? Admittedly, understanding Ukraine isn't an easy thing. We often don't understand our country either. However, it must – it simply must! – be pretty apparent that Ukrainians were driven to the Maidan in 2013 not by political manipulation, hunger, nationalism, or some egoistic interests, but by the same dream, as East Germans in 1989. Sadly, it isn't apparent at all to the outside world.

We Ukrainians think our country is yet another branch growing on the free and democratic tree called "United Europe". Well, Europe doesn't always see it that way. Partly, skepticism roots in Ukraine's chronic illnesses – like corruption and irresponsible, immature political elite. But mainly, it's about something else. Eastern Germans went with the flow. We go against it. They were rattling at the wall that was crumbling on its own. We are up against a wall that doesn't crack up so far. The time of bridges is on hold, leaving Europe's political scene once again defined by barriers.

The European Union weakens. NATO is split-up. Russia is full of itself and has a big mouth, but also—a shrinking economy. Its society is ill and—most importantly—not interested in therapy. China is strong and economically omnipresent, but remains a closed book for the West. As to the United States … American news is reminiscent nowadays of a surreal TV show. Whether it's a mini-series or an endless, dull, self-destructive mix of "The Apprentice" and "House of Cards" — remains to be seen.

Where is Ukraine's place in this world of crumbling principles and ghostly perspectives? The answer consists of two parts: internal and external. Internally, Ukraine's place in the world will be defined depending on her successful or unsuccessful reforms. We may be closer to success than we usually think. The number of people sizing Ukraine up as a next investment destination is rather substantial. No, they haven't decided yet, because … Because of the war.

The volume of new groundbreaking laws, the number of the new people in the government, the will to change, the curbed down bureaucracy, the level of freedom and creativity in the air—these positive factors are there in Ukraine. The situation is far from perfect, but there's enough solid ground to enable a leap forward. The heaviest impediment between today's Ukraine and a breakthrough is the lingering war in Donbas. And precisely because we are close to success, the Russian Federation does everything at its power to convince itself and us that Ukraine is heading to an abyss. And precisely because the war stands between us and success, Russia isn't in a hurry to end it. Nevertheless, I am sure: the war can be ended.

As soon as the words "Ukraine" and "war" aren't used in the same sentence anymore, as long as the war stops, the investments will come. Re-phrasing "The Field of Dreams" — "Stop it, and they will come!" It would be the one case where the modern Western "pragmatism" would be to our advantage. There are two things investors are keen upon: whether Ukrainians are ready to roll up their sleeves and whether the investment climate is there. Ukrainians are hard, honest workers. Have always been. And the investment climate is, step by step, coming around. What remains is getting rid of the curse of war and our status as a toxic country where too many economic projects have been bogged down over the last decades.

Now, to the external answer. Of course, you can't stop being what you are. Russia won't stop being a predator. Europe won't stop being an idea that ignites human hearts — the idea of freedom and democracy as the path to peace and prosperity. As long as this idea isn't proved wrong, the European Union won't lose its importance for Ukraine. That's why the Kremlin, subtle in many other things, is so brutal and blunt in its effort to discredit the idea of the united, democratic, free, tolerant, and prosperous Europe (or, as they elegantly put it, "Gayropa").

It's rather obvious that the EU wants to reconcile with Moscow. Sooner or later, it probably will. Further on in history, it will be extra cautious not to make Russia mad and inflame any new confrontation. The "64-thousand-dollar" question though is this: to what kind of compromise will the EU commit itself? Ukraine is Europe's historical test. I don't expect Europe to be conscientious to the end, but I do hope that, in the end, on the point of Ukraine, it chooses the right spot between confrontation and capitulation. And that this won't happen behind Ukraine's back. Also, I hope the EU is aware that even after it has reached a compromise on Ukraine with Russia — Moscow's attitude towards the West won't change. Not with the FSB/KGB elite running now the country. Which means: the confrontation will eventually flame up anew, in Ukraine or elsewhere.

The apparent threat to Ukraine is in Europe's growing trend towards nationalism. A mere glance at European politics of the last years makes this evident: nationalism isn't "love" (as it is presented on the election posters of the Ukrainian nationalist "Svoboda" party), but egoism. No one supports Putin more fervently in Europe than nationalists. Some of them don't even ignore Ukraine's pain, but rather enjoy it, as it helps prove their point: The United Europe is nothing but trouble, both for the EU and the neighborhood. The blinder Ukraine goes in her domestic disputes, the faster she goes down — the easier it will be for the nationalists of Europe to draw a line in the sand and to demand a different kind of a union for the continent (if any!).

Putin sees Europe's weakness as Russia's historic opportunity to change the European ship's course, to make it go astray from the transatlantic route. Which might push Europe over the edge in the direction of the new nationalism. Which, in turn, might make Russia a Gulliver in the European land of Lilliput. It's a legitimate scenario—but not the most likely one, as (unlike the Soviet Union) Russia simply lacks an idea that would make anyone—apart from political sellouts and nostalgic dictators—gravitate to it. Russia knows how to get into the heads of Europe's corrupt and weak, but lighting up the hearts of Europe's bright and strong has so far proved beyond its capability.

Therefore, politically diverse as it is, Europe (for Ukraine's purposes) can be divided into two camps: nationalistic and mainstream. The mainstream is all over the place now, but once Ukraine gets her act together, the European support will grow. On the other hand, European nationalism will fervently push us out of United Europe into the embrace of "the Russian world"—as this is where they see us.

The good news though is that Europe's nationalists have the same weakness as Putin's Russia: they aren't good at shaping a positive future. Or any future, for that matter. They can barely see the EU alive in a 10–15 years span. They have barely made their peace with Bulgaria's and Romania's EU accession. Wait till they tragically lament the Western Balkans knocking on the EU's door in a couple of years! Let's not scare them too much with the idea that Ukraine might come in next. What really counts is our success, conviction, and sense of destination. We know we belong to a United Europe. Europeans who care for the EU will get used to the idea of Ukraine's accession sooner or later, too.

It goes without saying that Europe's perseverance isn't enough to make sure the Western world doesn't crumble. America remains a big unknown, holding many unanswered questions. In his above-mentioned article, "Liberal world order, RIP!", Richard N. Haas gave a devastating diagnosis of the mental state of the West: the elites are losing their touch with the people. In other words, one of America's brightest minds states: at this critical juncture of history, when Russian leadership has full control of its citizens, the West has become a nervous wreck, whose head is at odds with its body. What an ideal breeding ground for populism! What a window of opportunity for Putin! Let's hope that Dr. Haas's article is just a warning; that his pessimism is overblown and that after a number of elections, the West's head will reconcile with its body. Otherwise, get ready for even more darkness in the world.

What should Ukraine do? Once again: count on herself. Be under no illusions about the West. Yet remember: "times they are a-changing". Heroic times get replaced with cowardly ones and vice versa. Our way is difficult but right. Two keys to Europe are already in our hands: the association agreement and the visa-free travel. And — even more important! — we have the support of many decent, sincere, courageous Europeans, and Americans. What remains is the "small" matter of our national ability to show with concrete deeds and ratings, with our faith and goodwill, that democratic Ukraine is a good economic growth space for Europe and the United States. At least not worse than the undemocratic "Russian world". Once we get there — global tides might turn either.

Battle for Europe.
Battle for the Soul

When the Ukrainian newspaper Dzerkalo Tyzhnya (DT) a while ago invited me to write a political forecast for Ukraine and Europe, I immediately had to think of Woody Allen's joke: "It's hard to make predictions, especially about the future". Indeed, I believe one can't predict the future, but one can guess it. There is a whole mythology around the fact that from time to time, someone guesses right—a mythology wildly popular in Ukraine. Probably, nowhere else in the world will you meet as many people certain about who will win the next election, say, in the United States — and even eager to bet a jug of good beer on that. I made peace with this Ukrainian phenomenon a long time ago. In reality, of course, no one knows for sure what comes next. Here lies the beauty, the horror, and at the same time, the hope of our life. Therefore, I didn't write a "forecast" in a conventional sense, but rather focused on what I fear and what I hope for as a Ukrainian. Being humbly and painfully aware, though, that neither my fears nor my hopes would probably come true either. Life always finds a way to outsmart us all. Here are some of the ideas from my DT forecast.

In 2009, the director of the American Stratfor Institute George Friedman published a book titled "The Next Hundred Years,"[28] a bold attempt to anticipate the biggest events of the 21st century. Including, for instance, a great US-Mexican war in the 2080s to be won by America due to its superiority in … space rocket-carriers.

However, what really caught my eye was Friedman's forecast of United Europe unraveling in the first quarter of the century. For 2015–2025, he predicted a Ukraine-Russia crisis at first and then a full-blown Russia-EU clash over the Baltics. And he didn't see an optimistic outcome for either of these two conflicts. In his view, the EU wouldn't be able to survive the crisis, and its leftovers would be divided in zones of influence among the new European

---

28 https://en.wikipedia.org/wiki/The_Next_100_Years:_A_Forecast_for_the_21 st_Century

superpowers: Germany, Poland, and Turkey. In a word, he thinks of tomorrow's Europe in terms of mayhem, war, and return to deep division lines.

Well ... Let's call it the "plan B". Despite the fact that Friedman was right predicting a major explosion between Ukraine and Russia, I can hardly imagine a major backslide to the wilder times in the EU and a dissolution of the idea that got so deeply absorbed in Europe's blood. Although, admittedly, Europe's devils from World War One and World War Two didn't go anywhere. They only have been asleep. As it appears now, they aren't anymore. The devil-whisperer in the Kremlin is blowing his horn — and all the nationalists, radicals, and political freaks in Europe creep out from their holes, thinking their time has come. So far, they are where they belong — on the margin of political life. Yet judging from the experience of other countries, the tables can turn quite fast. No doubt, Putin counts on it.

Let's not dwell on apocalyptic scenarios any longer than they deserve though. Europe's "Plan A" is the continuation of the United Europe project, in one form or another. United Europe was an unprecedented breach with the historical tradition. Overcoming century-long hatreds, rallying around liberal values, stopping wars, forgiving each other, focusing on the common future, not on past grievances — all this made the EU the noblest project to ever emerge from the world of politics. The beauty of the project was in its magnanimity. Sadly, magnanimity can also be its curse.

United Europe was built in the footsteps of the "great society" in the United States. In the 1960s, a personal car, a house, and a decent vacation became a reality for millions American households. A bit later, somewhere around the early 1970s, the mass prosperity finally reached Europe's middle class, too. Ever since, Europeans, self-conscious and energetic, have been rushing from one success to another. That's how they entered the turn of times in the early 1990s. Who would have thought that behind this turn, the elegant European sedan would encounter a rugged Russian KAMAZ ...

In the early 1990s, Russia was either written off as a beaten adversary or seen as a European perspective partner. In reality, it became neither. You can become a partner, only if you want to be one. Alas, Russia, incapable of dropping its zero-sum thinking, never really wanted that. And as to being "beaten" — an adversary isn't really beaten, and the war isn't really finished as long as he doesn't see himself beaten and the war finished. In Russia's mind, the confrontation with the West was never over.

No, the Cold War never ended — it was just on pause at first before it entered a stage where one side was leading it, while the other one was oblivious to it. Meanwhile, under President Vladimir Putin, Russia became the anti-thesis of Europe's impulse of uniting around shared values and leaving national animosity in the past. Russia couldn't care less about or think lower of United Europe's "common values". This attitude is literally put on display every night in Russia's leading political talk-shows. The Kremlin's thinking is based on (a) the notion of taking back what once was theirs and (b) questioning Europe's premise that respect to every human being comes before the interests of the state. It's a liberal, free Europe vs. paternalistic and revanchist one. After all, what is some "human being" compared to Mother Russia?

After President Yeltsin's voluntary withdrawal from the political scene, Russia got swept away with the idea of "Eurasianism". Putin's advisor Vladislav Surkov poetically interpreted it as "the loneliness of a half-blood."[29] Meaning that Russia is Europe and Asia simultaneously, a geopolitical half-blood, and therefore is destined to go its own way. This ideology rejected any notion of social progress and stipulated Russia's path as a mystical, irrational one, connecting Russians to the Kremlin and the Kremlin to God. Every reform is seen as the West's effort to expand, to change Russia's nature. I.e., an infringement on Eurasian space, an act of aggression on the West's part and of treason on the part of those Russians who want their country to become a better nation.

In the eyes of Eurasianists, Russia can't be changed, full stop. There can be only one kind of Russia in the world. And if this kind of Russia ceases to exist, then, using Putin's ominous expression, "why would we need this kind of a world?". Putin and his KGB pals put into Russian heads the notion that the one and only right

---

29   https://globalaffairs.ru/articles/odinochestvo-polukrovki-14/

relationship between the people and the government is the pater-nalistic one: give us power – and we will give you happiness.

At many points, Putin indeed excelled at selling happiness to his people. After all, what was Crimea's annexation, if not the hap-piness of a theft, a triumph over someone who is seen as weak and unworthy? Or what are Putin's daily political propaganda shows, if not the sheer happiness of seeing yet another "Ukrainian guest" or "Western pundit" humiliated, insulted and sometimes even smacked on the head publicly on live TV? And what is Russian propaganda if not the happiness of self-affirmation through some-one's humiliation? Yes, this kind of happiness is dark and slimy, but what are you going to do if you don't have any other kind to sell?

Putin gave Russians the joy of simple answers to difficult questions. Whose fault is it? – America's! Why are we great? – Be-cause we are large! Why are we entitled to what we do? – Because we are a superpower! And so, at the outset of the new century, pure darkness, intellectual trash, that would be humiliating in any other kind of situation, descended on the world's largest nation as its state ideology.

From classical Russian literature, we know Russia's "two om-inous questions". First – "Who is at fault?" Second – "What can be done (to fix it)?" In reality, both Ukraine and Russia face one and the same ominous question: "After being given so much by nature and geography – why are we so poor?" Paradoxically enough, de-spite historical proximity and apparent similarity, these two na-tions chose diametrically opposite answers.

Ukraine chose the hard and painful truth: it's all on us. It's all our own fault, and, if we want to live better, we need to change. Ever since, Ukraine's way is marked by this instinctive desire to change, to atone for her sins, to become a better nation (in the mold of the more successful Eastern Europeans). It's a difficult way. The desire is not always backed by the deeds of those at power. Many Ukrainians have despaired. On top of everything, Ukraine's chaotic democracy became a problem for many in Europe, whereas for many in Russia, Ukraine became an enemy. Let's face it, this kind of democracy, messy and complicated, is at this point, not Ukraine's greatest selling point. The noble dream hasn't made most Ukrainians richer or happier yet. Many Europeans would breathe a sigh of relief if Ukraine overnight peacefully and voluntarily joined "the Russian world". Russians would be ecstatic. And yet, Ukraine doesn't give up and stubbornly walks the way she chose.

In turn, Russia gave a different answer, a proud and happy one: it's all on "them". Yes, we are poor, but that's because someone else did it to us. To make things worse, this "someone" wanted us to change. Yet we are who we are; changing is beneath us.

Choosing a comfortable lie over the painful truth is a moral option of another kind — and Russia availed itself on it rather generously. While the Soviet Union saw the line between good and evil, but mixed them up, Vladimir Putin's Russia doesn't see the line at all. For Putin, the world is an inherently evil, dog-eat-dog place, in which Russia has no other choice but to play by the world's rules. Russians eagerly followed their leader into a world where the good is replaced with "the possible", and with an ideology of "pragmatism" — in Russia's case, a euphemism covering up the cult of force, rejection of moral and intoxicating permissiveness.

Putin prescribed his country a mental and emotional diet that only sounds simple, but really isn't. It offers not just simple answers, but a different set of simple answers for each audience. One kind for TV-watchers; another for those who get their information from YouTube. One kind for the young; another for the old. One kind for Russia; another for Europe; and yet another for America. On top of that, the emergence of social media made the global subconscious, the dusty attic (or basement) of international political thinking, more accessible. Russia dove into this new dimension of media faster than others. In many ways, it "owns" social media now.

Strictly speaking, on most occasions, Russian propaganda doesn't sell a lie, but rather an alternative reality, in which many things are true, and everything is rather interconnected logically. With one major correction: its framework is sheer delusion, as the "enemy at the gate", the fundamental premise of this version of reality, doesn't exist. In the last three decades, the West's preoccupation was mostly about building a peaceful, profitable win-win world, with Russia being an integral part of it. The idea was to somehow integrate Russia into the fiber of the new Europe.

Had Russia shown any kind of inclination to become a part of the EU—it would have received a perspective. Had Russia ever really wanted a mutually respectful relationship with the West—it would have had it. Yet, I never heard Russian politicians discuss it even with a slightest degree of earnestness. For Moscow, any kind of a win-win world was nothing short of a humiliation. Putin dreamt on a different level and a different time dimension: getting back into the global game, taking revenge for the fall of the Soviet Union, weakening the West and dividing the world anew.

Russia needed the "enemy at the gate" for ideological purposes—and it put it together, piece by piece. Those familiar with Soviet science fiction will recognize similarities with the iconic plot from the Arkadiy and Boris Strugatsky dystopian novel "The Inhabited Island"—with the fictional "fire-carrying fathers" as the real-life Kremlin, with the fictional "emanating towers" as the real-life omnipresent 24/7 propaganda and with the fictional "despicable degenerates" as the real-life Russian opposition. No wonder this novel's adaptation was one of the most successful in recent years in the Russian movie theaters.

Interestingly enough, the West itself starts to believe that it was all along … well if not "the enemy at the gate", then at least guilty of neglecting Russia's "legitimate interests" in the region. And therefore—complicit in Russia's turn to authoritarianism. Putin doesn't mind. Slowly, but surely, he drags the West into his own eschewed version of Europe's newest history, in his own reality. Simultaneously he separates Europe from America and America from Europe (blaming some things on America's "hubris" and others on Europe's "liberal nonsense").

He offers Europe simple answers, too. Why do I live below my expectations?—Because the money goes to the new EU member states! Why can't my child find a job?—Because the refugees took them! Why do we have sanctions on Russia?—Because Americans made us! Why is there a war in Ukraine?—Because they are fascists!

And once again, it works. The simple alternative reality fills up Europeans minds like sweet bubble-gum, creating a sense of intellectual satiety, selling to people the most comfortable version of themselves and the world around them. The version that applies to them the least possible pressure and makes any kind of sacrifice unnecessary. The only thing that counts in this reality is the new brave world's idol: "pragmatism". As we have seen in previous chapters, this idol has many faces. In this particular case, one can condense it to two words: "me first."

Europe's (and Ukraine's!) most dangerous seduction today is a dictatorship. Totalitarianism is a kind of "happiness" too. The love to the leader, the triumph of force, the euphoria of unity, the sense of overwhelming, intoxicating national pride—all these things Putin has successfully sold to Russians. Now he's trying to sell them to the West. After all, what is a democracy, if not a rather tiresome undertaking, where reforms can drown in decade-long political debates and where strategic thinking beyond the electoral cycle is almost impossible? On the other hand, I have seen a 2013 poll from a very decent EU country (which should remain unnamed), indicating that around 60% of its population wouldn't mind giving almost absolute power to a strong, competent leader not dependent on elections or parliament. In other words, if you don't call a dictatorship by its name, the majority might like it. So, don't be too surprised when you hear from Europeans, "we wish we had someone like Putin." Russian propagandists have in Europe both a field and a human material to work with. As I stated before, Europe's demons aren't gone. They have just been asleep for a while—but aren't anymore.

While Russia was emerging as an alternative Europe, the European Union was emerging as a bulwark in the way of Putinism. Take a look at the political landscape, and you'll see it rather clearly. Not everyone who is for the EU is opposed to Putin, but the absolute majority of those opposed to the EU stand for Putin. In the brave new world of today, everything amoral, egoistic, indifferent in Europe rallies under the banners of nationalism—and takes on the EU. Putin grows to a kind of "uber-nationalist" of the continent. Ukraine has her own story with nationalism—it will be a separate topic in the chapter "Why nationalism cannot be the idea of European Ukraine."

Ukraine's "European perspective", flimsy as it is at this point, might nevertheless be the thread that leads the country out of the Labyrinth. At least, that's the one ideological notion, time-tested success model we can hold on to right now. Of course, at this point in our and Europe's history, it's not as much about ideology as about economic success, which is up to us and no one else. We would have to become economically successful first to get integrated second — not combine the two things simultaneously, as was the case with our Eastern European neighbors. Same goal; different path. A much more difficult one, considering that Ukraine's EU integration isn't much of an issue in today's Europe.

Ukraine's selling point (aside from the fertile land, the mild climate, the developed infrastructure, the proximity to the EU, and the educated population) is that, unlike Russia, we don't make an idol out of our past sins and of who we are right now. We are ready to learn from others. We are ready to roll up our sleeves. We are ready to start at zero and even at the minus (considering how much credit of trust Ukraine was granted and has wasted in her first three decades of independence). We don't need to live a lie. We want to and can live in truth. There is so much talent and selflessness in our people (just take a look at the volunteer movement in the war years!). All the parts of success are there — we just need to put them together.

Our angry Ukrainian political talks in the kitchen, our depressive political talk-shows, our despair at our electoral choices — isn't this a collective redemption on the way to our dream of becoming a better nation? Ukrainians want it so bad that they had two revolutions within one decade. Where else would that be even thinkable?

Take a look at Facebook. In the West, it's mostly about posting family pictures and congratulating each other on birthdays. In Russia, it's all about manipulating, heating up, and cooling down the masses. And in Ukraine ... in Ukraine, it's all about endless political battles among Ukrainians about the fate of their country. This kind

of passion — on- and offline — could be a big thing, if used construc-
tively. If only our ethos would catch up to our pathos!

Year after year, we keep making noise, pouring our national
soul out, but our talk is clearly bigger than our walk. This doesn't
necessarily mean that Ukraine won't handle its historic issues eventually — primarily the issues of trust, our complicated relationship
with truth. We still see the top tier of society living in lies and corruption — and often feel entitled to do likewise (if *they* are doing it,
why can't *we*?). But the opposite can be the case too. If someone at
the top, year after year, infects Ukraine with their lawlessness,
someone at the top can become Ukraine's inspiration, also.

Once this "someone" shows a good example and finds the
right words — the masses will catch on. Not immediately, but eventually. Corruption is nothing but a bad habit, like smoking. Decency
can be a habit, too. I see a growing number of decent, pro-Western,
pro-European people in key positions within the government. Even
the hopelessly corrupt ones try to be better. We witness the birth of
something that wasn't there before: the culture of honest and professional public service in Ukraine. In a way, it's a normal human
reaction amid a lingering war: feeling shame, trying to live up to
your nation who has sacrificed so much.

Of course, bad habits die hard: dilettantism of those in charge,
our chronic inability to believe in anything and anybody. Ukrainian
souls are the battlefield between good and evil — just like Ukrainian
politics. An Austrian friend of mine once compared Ukraine to a
teenager who got abused as a child and doesn't believe anybody
ever since. He might be onto something here. After century-long
existence in limbo between Europe and Russia, after the 1932–33
artificial hunger, after the two world wars, after Chornobyl, Crimea, and Donbas — Ukraine needs to be treated like a teenager, who
survived horrors and who needs help in getting back to normal life.
Patiently, but most importantly — truthfully and humbly.

Now, back to George Friedman's idea of United Europe unraveling and getting divided among the national states. I partly as-
cribe this anticipation to the silent euro-skepticism I occasionally
encounter among my American friends. Those familiar with the
United States would confirm: in the eyes of many (especially

conservative) Americans, the EU looks suspiciously "pink", liberal. Many don't believe in this project's durability. Yet, those familiar with the EU would disagree and argue that Europe's inner core is strong enough to overcome its growing domestic challenges.

I ask myself though: is it strong enough to deal with an external adversary, who knows Europe's weak spots and is ready to patiently split, fool and push the EU until it falls? Russia will be a challenge to Europe at least equal in magnitude to the refugee crisis and all kinds of financial meltdowns. Russia is getting into Europe's head, eroding its self-respect, just like it has undermined Ukraine's ability to believe in itself. One by one, it tries to pull EU's neighbors into the Russian zone of influence. If things keep going this way, Friedman's notion of a "battle for the Baltics" wouldn't be so far-fetched. Yet the main prize isn't the Baltics, but Ukraine. And the battle for Ukraine is roaring on for years.

If Putin succeeds in crushing the Ukrainian revolution and independence, a new Ukraine will arise in the EU's direct vicinity. Not a Poland #2, as anticipated, but a Haiti #2. The continent would be thoroughly destabilized for decades. Suppressing Ukraine's resistance (and it would have to be suppressed daily), Russia would grow furthermore radicalized — and the EU would complete its transformation into a closed club. "Closed" both in the sense of pulling the plug on the EU enlargement, and in the sense of dropping the European idea as a transformational factor, and in the sense of having to deal with the unstable, and evermore wild "East" on a daily basis.

This region would then stop being the growth space for democracy and become the petri dish for dictatorships. The gloomy script of the Strugatsky brothers can become a full-blown dystopia of the Wachowski sisters, in which walking the thin line between the hot and cold war would prove even more challenging than in the times of the Berlin Wall. Therefore, it's vital that the EU takes this doom-and-gloom scenario seriously enough — as well as avoids the strategic missteps that could lead into the abyss (like building the NordStream-2 pipeline).

The EU isn't just a political project, but a tipping point in history. The moment where nations learned how to break the historic vicious cycle of hatred and wars. The Union did the impossible: made values more important than borders, elevated politics above national egoism. Yet, as was stated before, the EU is facing an opponent now who is not magnanimous, but vengeful and far from seeing the world in win-win categories. This opponent is becoming a kind of alternative Europe, attractive to some Europeans. His goal is dividing the continent anew and putting the law of force above the force of law. At least in the part of the world that Russia sees as its "jurisdiction".

Is United Europe ready to call things by their names and defend itself? Apparently, not quite. By forcefully changing borders, by meddling with other nations' elections, by poisoning Putin's enemies and conducting malicious propaganda—Russia is pushing the envelope farther and farther, exploring how far it can go. In a way, it's slowly heating the pot, hoping that the EU gets "cooked" without even noticing it. It would be a pity if the noble European drive would fizzle out like that. And of course, it would be the worst-case scenario for Ukraine and a historical emasculation to Europe in general.

The EU duly sees itself as a powerful tool of positive transformation, turning enemies into friends. It's not in the EU's nature to look for enemies or even for ways to coexist with enemies. It has been EU's strong suit all along. However, now this can be its weakness—as Russia isn't keen to peacefully coexist. At least as long as it doesn't have its piece of the global pie back.

Ukraine's dilemma is the same as Europe's: how do you live next to a paranoid, aggressive neighbor without plunging into a major war? What kind of compromise is legitimate, and what kind of compromise is unacceptable? In one word: how to live next to Putin's Russia? It's a Ukrainian and European question without a definitive answer. An honest answer means political hell. A dishonest one—Russia's victory. And a lack of an answer means that Ukraine will keep losing her best sons and daughters in the war, and the EU will keep losing its drive and credibility. In the end, it's not about the right political calculation, but about the soul of Europe. If Russia wins, the EU's reputation as the project that represented a tipping point of history will be confirmed — but in an evil, doom-spelling rather than redemptive sense.

The battle for Europe's soul goes on — hot and bloody inside Ukraine, cold and cynical outside her. My prediction is: someone will win; a draw is not likely.

Why Nationalism Can't Be the Idea
of a European Ukraine

I understand why Europe's dead-eyed "pragmatists" are suspicious of Ukraine. But what about the people at the other ideological end — the European idealists? Why don't these ageless, forever young "boys" and "girls" with burning eyes and unbreakable ideals picket Russian embassies worldwide demanding the immediate release of political prisoners, as they did during Soviet times? Why do we see them so often on Putin's side and not on Ukraine's?

Ideologically, the key reason is the paradox, the contradiction that for a while has been hanging over Ukraine: how do you build a European (i.e., internationalist) project on our typically Ukrainian mix of internationalist desires and nationalist slogans, backgrounds? While Europe's nationalists don't accept us because we refuse to bow to Europe's uber-nationalist Putin, Europe's mainstream politicians are often extra cautious around us because they see us as nationalists.

Accordingly, if we want to see the mainstream segment of Europe's politics on our side, we can't be nationalists. Jokingly or not — we often say we are. But are we really? Do we invest this word with the same meaning as an average pro-EU European? In most cases — we don't. At least, this is not what I see among my friends. Most pro-EU Ukrainians (and according to surveys, it's a majority of the population) are far from nationalistic thinking, in the form and shape as Europe understands this phenomenon. They confuse or misappropriate the two classic political terms: nationalism and patriotism, the two worldviews that are as close and distant, as courage and obsession, pleasure and addiction. Being a patriot means loving your country. Being nationalist means being unwilling to share your country with those who belong to it, but aren't like you.

The problem dates back to the time between the end of World War Two and the Soviet Union's downfall — a period that we Ukrainians, and the Western Europeans have spent somewhat differently, to say the least. The generation of Ukrainians who spent a part of their life in the USSR (primarily, people of my age and the generation of my parents) grew up seeing the ideology of internationalism as something deeply Soviet, i.e., insincere, artificial, anti-Ukrainian. On the other hand, nationalism was, in our eyes, the slogan of the anti-Soviet resistance. We are used to seeing nationalism as something coming from the heart, courageous, revolutionary, and selfless — akin to Mel Gibson's character in "Braveheart." Mainstream Europe views this ideology in a different light — more like the real-life Mel Gibson. Often confused and with anger management issues.

The western (mainly European) world, with which Ukraine wants to integrate, is, for the most part, based on the ideas of internationalism and solidarity of nations. This world was actively cocreated by social-democrats, joined after 1968 by the greens and other political forces of the left spectrum. For this world, the word "nationalism" has a profoundly negative, anti-EU connotation. The same goes for the majority of Europe's centrists and even conservatives. For them, nationalism is something that dominated Europe for centuries, brought immeasurable suffering, and culminated in two world wars. It's something with which Europe parted ways in 1945, hopefully for good.

Of course, nationalism does exist in this world, along with nationalist philosophers, artists, politicians, and even heads of states. Yet, this doesn't change the basic truth: both United Europe and the transatlantic world are, for the most part, political projects, rejecting nationalism as the "original sin" of the West.

In the Western world, nationalist thinking clashes with mainstream thinking, and the nationalist idea is the antithesis of the concept of a United Europe. The moment when the nationalist forces take over the European and transatlantic world (and they are indeed on the rise right now) will be the end of the European and transatlantic projects as we know them. Hoping for such an outcome or working to that end would be the most absurd notion for a country like Ukraine. United Europe can be replaced only with a world where surviving (let alone succeeding) would be way more difficult for Ukraine than it is right now.

This is today's background. One doesn't need to get into a fight about whether this background is good or bad (although, in my view, a united, solidary, and internationalist Europe is the best environment for a nation that for centuries was forced to exist in limbo and wants to pave her way back to the European scene). Let's just take it as a given.

It makes no sense explaining to Europe the difference between good and bad nationalism (most of my Ukrainian friends think it exists and it's important for Europe to understand it). European integration is merely the process of adopting European standards, narratives, lexicon — and not of amending them by every new member. To a certain extent, as long as we aren't a member, it's a one-way street. As Ivan Krastev says, we imitate Europe in the hope of becoming one. At this stage of Ukraine's history, it's a binary choice: either we say we are Europeans, or we say we are nationalists. Saying "We are European nationalists" (like we often do) means "We are European, but we don't really need the European Union". This is, by the way, how many centrist and left politicians in Europe do see us.

We look absurd, when, on the one hand, knock on the EU's door and on the other — question its tolerance culture, PC language, historical memory, etc. We need to understand: European integration isn't just about joining a bigger market and a world of prosperity, but rather a transition into a world that has its own language and values that, in turn, bring prosperity. Let's be honest: despite our heartfelt pro-European enthusiasm, we have a blurry understanding of what Europe is. We haven't yet really comprehended either the scope or the gist of this new world that we want to enter.

Europe's morality isn't just based on the distinction between good and evil, but rather between good, evil, and absolute evil. For instance, Stalinism is in Europe's eyes evil, but not absolute evil. Absolute evil is Nazism/Fascism/Neo-Nazism. For United Europe, the absolute evil is what Hitler did to Europe in general and to the Jewish people in particular in 1933–45. Which doesn't mean that we Ukrainians should in any way or form tolerate Stalinism or communism.

Some EU countries, based on their individual history, did find a legitimate ideological corner for these radically left ideologies. Today's Europe has enough political space and understanding even for Trotskyites. This doesn't mean that we Ukrainians have to do the same. A mere look at our history is enough to realize: Ukraine is fully entitled to see Stalinism as absolute evil, conducting a zero-tolerance policy towards Stalin's "legacy" and his crimes, just as much as towards Hitler and his crimes.

Zero tolerance means being 100% serious about certain manifestations of evil, even in the smallest dosage. For instance, in United Europe, sentences that start with the words "At least Hitler built good highways …" are unthinkable and extremely offensive. Just like posting a "Heil Hitler" picture "to troll Russians". Just like using any deprecating, diminishing names to refer to any nationality and ethnicity. All these things are signs of belonging to a civilization different than European (or, rather to no civilization at all).

These aren't jokes. They aren't funny. And they definitely aren't covered by the "freedom of speech" clause. Once again: it's not something to discuss or prove or argue with. In the European "universe", it's as elementary as washing hands or not littering on the street. It's a European, Western immunity, hygiene, and daily philosophy created to prevent Nazism's disaster once and for all. Since this hygiene, for some reason, wasn't instilled with the Soviet people in the post-World War Two time, we need to start with the basics. I.e., with the codex of rules, adopted via the behavior of the elites, via education, via a system of punishment and encouragement. We need to grow up as a nation—not for someone else, but for ourselves.

Admittedly, in the Pew Research survey of the level of anti-Semitism in Europe in 2016, Ukraine stood rather well compared to other post-Soviet countries and even some EU members.[30] On top of that, the very fact that an ethnic Jew, Volodymyr Zelenskyi, was elected Ukraine's president by a landslide in 2019 speaks volumes. And nevertheless …

---

30   https://ukrainianjewishencounter.org/en/news/anti-semitism-in-europe-uk
raine-turns-out-to-be-the-most-friendly-to-jews/

It's unimaginable in Europe that a group of rightwing skinheads would celebrate Hitler's birthday by beating a Jewish student half to death and get away with a hooliganism charge—as happened in Dnipropetrovsk in 2006. It's unimaginable in Europe that a synagogue would be demonstratively desecrated on a Christmas Eve—and the state wouldn't even issue a statement of condemnation—as took place in Odesa in 2017. Yes, one might describe these as single incidents—but, like any dangerous symptom, they can become something immensely bigger if not appropriately treated at the right time. And we Ukrainians have some learning to do in that department. The government must be principled and uncompromised in fighting all forms of xenophobia—and educate citizens accordingly. The concept of "hate crime" must be explained and indoctrinated in citizens from childhood. The line between good, evil, and absolute evil must be drawn with unmistakable clarity—for all our sakes.

The same goes for the "Aryan symbolic" of the regiment Azov in Donbas, for the racial views of the Right Sector and for the National Corps trying to patrol the streets of our cities. The choice is straightforward: either staying in this blurry archaic world of controversial political and historical allegiances or entering the European world. No one questions the heroism of the Azov fighters, who liberated Mariupol from Russia, or the sacrifice of Vasyl Slipak, who fought for Ukraine as a part of the Right Sector. It's obvious that a renowned European opera singer Slipak had nothing to do with the racist views of the Right Sector founders. I also think that most Azov fighters have barely heard of the social-nationalist roots of this regiment. Yet Europe's zero-tolerance policy towards anything pertaining to Nazism/Fascism/Neo-Nazism confronts Ukraine with a choice: either distance ourselves clearly from this kind of rhetoric, ideology and symbolic—or face an isolated existence with zero chances of ever belonging to a United Europe.

In other words, the problem isn't just Europe often not hearing Ukraine, but Ukraine often not hearing Europe—over meaningful, ideological issues, that is. Ukraine often doesn't really understand or doesn't really take to heart what matters most to Europe and therefore doesn't adopt the European codex of behavior.

Depending on whether we start hearing Europe, whether our thinking and rhetoric evolve over years, Ukraine will or will not get a chance for a new, more positive future among friends. I.e., civilized countries who live by the rules, have a clear distinction between good and evil — and don't stab you in the back, as Russia did in 2014.

Ukraine, the Church and the Post-Truth World

Fair warning: this will be a dark chapter. Maybe the darkest in the book. The chapter on Ukraine's relation with trust. The confusion between nationalism and patriotism is Ukraine's problem, but not her biggest sin. Ukrainians part ways with Russia not because they are nationalists or because they are so much better, but because they see in Russia the reflection of what they want to get rid of: injustice, despotism, the indulgence of the strong, humiliation of the weak ... Russia has put its sins on a pedestal and reveres them. Well, in a way, it's their right and their moral choice. Empires always have this privilege: to look into a moral abyss and call it "our special way". Ukraine doesn't enjoy and doesn't need this kind of "privilege". She sees Putin's Russia, with its hypocrisy, lies, and cruelty, for what it is — an abyss.

Strictly speaking, it's not as much Ukraine splitting with Russia, as Russia breaking up with civility. This split has been happening for quite a while. Most memorably — in March 2014, when Russia madly, with drunken tears of happiness, was celebrating the Crimean triumph over defenseless Ukraine. Weeks later, came the dark day of April 13, 2014, the Palm Sunday, when the ex-FSB officer, Russian citizen Igor Girkin "minced" (in his own words) the officer of Ukrainian Security Service Gennadiy Bilichenko in Donbas. Yes, when reporting ambushing and killing of a Ukrainian officer, the first combat victim of the Russia-Ukraine war, Girkin used the word "minced", like he was talking about meat or a piece of broccoli. This was the moment of truth: we Ukrainians were nothing but meat for Putin's goons from the get-go. If someone is looking for the tipping point in Ukraine-Russia relations — take a close look at the day when the war started!

Yet, this chapter isn't as much about "them", as about us. With the Ukrainian orthodox church drifting away from the Russian omophorion (and this process is in full motion since 2018), we are no longer bound to Moscow's spiritual compass. From now on, Ukraine's sins are Ukraine's sins. Not Russia's or anyone else's, but ours. We have no one to blame for what we decide, do or don't do.

Just like we have no one who would go our path of cleaning up our state and making it better.

Professor Timothy Snyder has a theory of hyper-typical Ukraine. He maintains that the 20th century Ukraine more than others reflected all the trends of those dramatic hundred years: from the failure of young national states in the face of empires to the deeply inhuman nature of the said empires. Later on, in his monograph "The Road to Unfreedom: Russia, Europe, America" Snyder deals, among other things, with the phenomenon of the so-called post-truth world — and shows that it came to the post-Soviet space earlier than to other parts of the world. In other words, in a way, both one hundred years ago and now, in today's world, Ukraine remains hyper-typical.

"The post-truth world" is a trendy concept, describing the mass delusion that truth doesn't really exist and must be replaced with interpretation, point of view, and impression that vary from person to person. Once the media adopt this view, their mission changes from establishing the facts to reflecting viewpoints. This is the warmest and bubbliest bath for an information consumer: it's up to him or her from there onwards to decide what is real and what isn't. Typically, and unsurprisingly, a person chooses the version of reality with which he or she is most comfortable. I.e., the one where he or she looks good and doesn't need to make too much effort. For a politician, it opens unlimited possibilities to be a conductor of a whole orchestra of human weaknesses, prejudices, and fears.

The post-truth world is indeed the most comfortable of all possible universes. Only upon taking a closer look, you realize the scary-simple thing: the post-truth world is a world without truth, a world of lies a la carte. For a faithful person, it's a world without God.

The consumer society eagerly and rather unwittingly slid into this new reality. Russia "owns" it, being not just its resident, but also the founding shareholder. Most people in the West are comfortable with it, too. The post-truth world gives them the privilege to detach themselves emotionally from what happens in places like Ukraine and Syria (who knows what is really going on there!) and still to feel good about themselves by donating five dollars a month for a hungry child in Africa. However, Professor Snyder is right: this mental plague isn't at work in the West only. The post-Soviet nations were among the first who got a taste of this brave new world.

Where is truth in the life of an average Ukrainian? Its place is usually in the kitchen, smoking room, or on Facebook. I.e., where it has no consequences. Traumatized by our history, we live with an a priori assumption that people can't be trusted, that any law can be manipulated, that "all politicians are thieves." This low spirit is to the post-truth world what manure is to ringworms. The lord of lies in the Kremlin couldn't wish for a better gift than the spirit of constant despair in Ukraine. It gives him the courage and confidence that Ukraine will disgust herself eventually, and slide into the abyss for good, sooner or later.

Let's be honest: we Ukrainians live in a world where political exposure for the most part brings no consequences; where a well-financed politician is unsinkable; where success is a priori seen with suspicion. An American dad sees an expensive car drive on the street and says to his child: learn good, work hard—and one day you'll afford it too. A Ukrainian dad would most likely say: look, there drives another bloodsucking cheater! In both cases, the parent says what history taught him—and the child listens and draws consequences for the rest of his or her life.

We are so used to living in a world of distrust and disbelief that even when something good happens, we convince ourselves it isn't happening to us. With the same zeal, we look for dark cats in the dark and the light rooms. We draw hopelessness like a scared child draws a blanket over his head. We are more used to pain than to joy. We don't expect the good outside our close circle—and if you don't expect the good, the good doesn't come.

Trust is the glue that ties society together. We have a considerable shortage of that. It always amazes me how a Western journalist would say, "according to my sources"—and no one doubts that these sources do exist and that they do claim what the journalist reports. A word can be enough to bring down a politician, to make him repent and redeem things. In Ukraine, a word has lost (or almost lost) its power. A politician can be caught red-handed, and yet — whoops, water off a duck! — he is still in the game; he still appears on political shows; he is still electable. Why? Because, "what else is new, we knew all along they were thieves".

Ukraine's spiritual leader, Reverend father Borys Gudziak, conducted a poll among the Ukrainian immigrants in Paris, asking, among other things, who people trusted and distrusted the most. Amazingly, Ukrainians in Paris distrust the most ... other Ukrainians in Paris. Just think about it. And no, it's not only about being trustworthy or untrustworthy — it's about the mood, the faith, the inner core of the nation that suffered too much and maybe didn't learn the right lessons from her history. Not yet.

Ukraine's sin is the sin of little faith. Including the little faith in ourselves, our country, our next ones. We know where it comes from. From a century-long existence in limbo. From the treason of politicians so richly dispersed all over our history. From the 1932–33 artificial mass starvation that went into history as Holodomor. From the Soviet leftovers so boldly plundered by Ukraine's politicians in the post-Soviet decades. From moral authorities so sorely missed in politics and society.

Yet, above all, our weakness comes from our daily, mundane decisions. From our silence, jealousy, egoism and greed. Let's keep this in mind when opening a new page of our national history. While walking away from the external (Russian) abyss, let's also move away from this internal moral swamp.

One of our time's most original minds, Ivan Krastev, describes the new type of a European citizen that can spell doom to the EU. "He wants change, but resents any form of political representation [...], he values disruption and scoffs at political blueprints. He longs for political community, but refuses to be led by others. He will risk clashing with the police but is afraid to trust any party or politicians."[31] Sounds familiar, doesn't it?

The post-truth world couldn't bring any other kind of character, but a somewhat infantile, disgruntled, distrustful individual. That's the hero of our time. And as he materialized in Ukraine

---

31   https://www.amazon.com/After-Europe-Ivan-Krastev/dp/0812249437, p. 85.

earlier than elsewhere, as we have amassed more experience with this character—maybe we also have a better chance of coming up with an antidote. It looked for a while as if this antidote was found in 2014. Under Russia's hideous attack, Ukrainians, these natural-born skeptics, this collective Doubting Thomas, all of a sudden, found their inner core and unity—went to the front to defend their country.

Standing apart from other European countries, Ukraine doesn't have much to lean upon in today's world. Krastev explains that with the fading from memory of the three historical pushes for European unification (the 1939–45 shock, the 1968 grassroots liberal revolution, and the 1989–91 unity drive between East and West),[32] the EU is becoming emotionally and substantially detached from its origins. It becomes hostage to the mega-problem of uncontrolled migration. It grows trivial and small-minded in its thinking and planning. Figuratively speaking, the banner of freedom might be folded and tied, like a rag, onto the EU's doorknob to keep the refugees (and new members) outside. Ideologically speaking, Krastev sees the United Europe of the coming years as a bleak shade of what it just recently used to be and what brought peace and prosperity to so many Europeans.

Well, a negative diagnosis is often the right one. However, let's hope not in this case. At least, many European elections of the last years showed a remarkable resilience on the part of the pro-European forces—and an electoral "ceiling" to the nationalistic ones. The banner of values might be dingy, but its place is still on the hoister and not on a doorknob.

The new elections in the coming years might boost nationalist forces in Europe—but I think they won't change their status of a marginal, destructive power, whose recipe for all problems is taking Europe back in time to what it used to be before the EU. Being on the margin of the political process is their designated place so far. The main threat to the European idea is not so much the rise of anti-European forces as the regeneration of pro-European ones.

---

32   https://foreignpolicy.com/2018/07/10/3-versions-of-europe-are-collapsing-at-the-same-time/

Their immunity to post-truth and to the cynicism disguised as "pragmatism" is visibly fading. For the foreseeable future, an ideologically weakening West will be the backdrop of world politics.

We Ukrainians often delude ourselves into explaining this phenomenon through the offense of Russian propaganda only. In reality, Moscow is just filling and expending the void emerging in the western minds as the euro-optimism ebbs away, and as the transatlantic partnership loses its gravity.

We are all submerged in the crisis of trust—Ukraine first, the West second. We believe less in ourselves; we rely less on our partners. It can't be just Moscow's doing. It's something more profound. We Ukrainians are not the ones to judge, but we are the ones to find our own way out of this quagmire. The West, in turn, has its own healing to undergo and explaining to do. Let's hope, someday it will come up with the explanation as to why in the first quarter of the 21st century its spirit all of a sudden flagged, and its moral compass went somewhat astray.

The global ideological vacuum is being filled with all kinds of mental junk food: conspiracy theories, nationalistic superstitions, the anarchism of "jillettes jaunes", Islamist fundamentalism ... The West, as we can see, draws its own darkness. The 20th century stubbornly doesn't want to end. Like a gigantic funnel, it drags Europe back into the war—with Russia's active help. A cold one at the least, a hot one in the worst case. I saw surveys, according to which most Germans, French and British see the continent on the brink of a major military confrontation. This premonition is clearly up Putin's alley. Fear combined with weakness is perfect playdough in the hands of a former KGB recruiter. What he can't deal with is courage combined with strength. When faced with a strong spirit, his best idea is poisoning people, jailing them and sending them beyond the polar circle, as he did with the prisoner of conscience Oleg Sentsov.

When holding his last word before Putin's "court", Sentsov used the famous Mikhail Bulgakov quotation: "There is no worse sin than cowardice." Courage is the one effective vaccine against the post-truth plague. United Europe will have to be courageous enough to take, at least partly, the blame for its moral and political crisis of today. It will have to face up the fact that the growing

European void, the estrangement between the elites and the "forgotten Europeans" was caused, among other things, by the political hubris of those at the top, which caused a lack of real dialogue with those in society who felt abandoned, lost and left behind.

United Europe will have to find the right approach to this "protest electorate" and stop shrugging off the questions that make the EU uncomfortable. For instance, about Europe's religious and national identity. Ukraine will probably have to undergo the same self-reflection—just much more of it, considering how many more in our society feel abandoned, forgotten and lost.

Both Ukraine and United Europe will need the same remedy: an honest domestic dialogue. The EU, with its relatively effective institutions and strong traditions, is moving in that direction. On the other hand, Ukraine is much slower, as its government isn't yet capable enough, and as it lacks any tradition of a domestic dialogue. The war in Donbas isn't helping either.

This is where the Ukrainian church can come in and help find answers to difficult existential questions. After all, isn't it the raison d'etre of any church—to look for inner peace, wisdom, and moral healing?

Within the last decades, Ukraine has constantly been looking for a new beginning. Chances have come and gone, but a real breakthrough escapes us. In early 2018, the rise of an independent Ukrainian Orthodox church led by a modern, relatively young prior, under the Mother-Church patronage in Constantinople, was yet another door opened to Ukraine by history. A faithful person would say another of God's blessings.

According to surveys, no one in Ukraine enjoys as much trust as the church. The tradition of strong religious leaders has existed here for quite a while. In the coming years, everything Metropolitan Epiphanius says will be heard. Let him not be silent. Let him find the right words for our society—so often deceived and, therefore, so often distrustful. Of course, it's also to be anticipated that Moscow will do its utmost to discredit both Epiphanius and the freshly-created church. Sadly, many Ukrainians (inclined to believe in anything but in their own country) will make it exceedingly easy.

Ukraine's independent orthodox church needs to do what a church does. Make the word mean something again. Bring trust back in our lives. Remind the strong that they aren't forever in this world and that the day will come when they will have to answer to God. Help the weak. Pray for those in the frontline. Encourage mercy for those who went astray under the influence of Russia. Help find peace amid the turmoil. Heal the wounds. Remind people that good always makes sense and that the failure is nothing but a decision every person makes for themselves.

Ukrainian leaders (spiritual and political) face a sea of despair and millions of souls looking for inner peace and answers to complicated questions. Moral and political. Politics usually doesn't answer such questions. It measures life in electoral cycles: from election to re-election. However, there must be someone who finally starts talking to Ukraine from the vantage point of history, maybe even eternity, life and death.

Erecting a Ukrainian independent church in the middle of a war, a church for skeptics and pessimists — what can be harder! At the same time, let's not forget that Doubting Thomas was a disciple too. God loves skeptics too. It is for a reason that the words "help my disbelief" can be heard in so many orthodox prayers. We can be as gloomy and pessimistic about our country as we want, but faithful people read in the Bible: what's impossible for a man is possible for God. And as to non-believers, they simply know: there must be a reason, why the Ukrainian nation survived whole epochs of historical coma, the horrific 20th century, and didn't waste away, like so many others in the course of history. There must be something special about these people, so often drowning and nevertheless surviving.

The Strasbourg Betrayal

Russia's unrepented return to the Parliamentary Assembly of the Council of Europe (PACE) in 2019 was expected – and yet came as a shock to most Ukrainians. Which showed one thing: Ukraine is in love with a Europe that doesn't exist anymore. When speaking of EU integration, we Ukrainians mean the EU of the late 1990s and early 2000s – i.e., the time when the idea of integrating the nations from Europe's East conquered European minds and hearts. It isn't the case anymore. The notion of the ever expanding and deepening European Union has drowned in a sea of new considerations, superstitions, and – most importantly – fears.

It's a different EU and a different Europe now. A one that doesn't know what comes next. A one that (let's face it) isn't particularly eager anymore to be a standard-bearer of good ideas (freedom, democracy, tolerance) to the outside world. It wants to have these ideas for itself – and the world can get along as it pleases. And yes, for some Europeans, Ukraine's freedom is almost as much of a nuisance as it is for Russia – as it stands between the EU and Russia, between the worlds of freedom and unfreedom that want to be friends again, shake hands and – most importantly! – conduct trade to mutual profit. That's the insane geopolitical twist in which Ukraine finds herself in the early 21st century.

Nevertheless, the European idea remains right for Ukraine. Moreover, it's our only way ahead. Not only because it's the alternative to all the evils embodied in today's Russia (and often reflected in today's Ukraine). There have been two templates in front of Ukraine for quite a while: that of Russia and that of Poland. Poland has been more convincing, to put it mildly. Its success has captivated, mesmerized the politically active part of Ukrainian society, Ukraine's brain and soul. Ukraine would rather be like Poland than Russia – especially, unsurprisingly after Russia burnt all bridges towards Ukraine in 2014.

Admittedly and obviously, living in freedom, Ukraine hasn't become successful yet – far from it. However, living in unfreedom isn't an option at all (as demonstrated via two Ukrainian revolutions within one decade). The key unanswered question is: what comes out of these revolutions, of this enormous national passion and drive that were aimed at making Ukraine a better nation, based on European principles? Well, slowly, but surely, we are on the way. However, there are several things we still have to realize.

For instance, Ukraine is yet to realize that European integration isn't an integration into prosperity, but integration into a system of values that brings prosperity. I.e., the rule of law, freedom of speech, mutual responsibility between the state and the citizen, tolerance to minorities, respect to other peoples and nations. How many of us Ukrainians (including the politically active part of the society) can sincerely say: yes, these are my values? How many of us value Europe for what it brings and not for what it is? How many of us want to arrive there without really moving there? These are the key questions we should ask ourselves, possibly daily.

One more thing that became evident in the wake of the "Strasbourg deal" of 2019: the European project is a project of trust. Ukraine's problem is: we haven't earned much trust with Europe so far. They don't see us as one of "them". It's our fault, not theirs. First, Ukraine did a lot to damage her own reputation. Second, do we trust ourselves enough to expect others to trust us? Third, maybe—who knows—we are indeed not 100% "one of them", but rather a different historical animal, the other part of free Europe. After all, the idea of personal freedoms that ripened in the rest of Europe over centuries has sprouted in Ukraine within a historically minuscule period, despite Ukraine's history and not as a logical conclusion of it. And—who knows—maybe this difference, this ability to move towards freedom against the flow of history, this rebellion against historical fate is the biggest reason why Europe should hold on to Ukraine. When history moves in the wrong direction (and it appears to be the case now), you need nations capable of defying it.

We Ukrainians haven't imitated freedom, but discovered it on our own and kept defending it as well as possible. Unlike the new EU members from the late 1990s and early 2000s, we move towards a Europe that is tired and skeptical, not pumped-up with serotonin and enthused. It's a dramatic real-life story of a nation that was given up, but refused to give up and is trying to catch up with United Europe — on her own, to the best of her abilities.

"The Spirit breathes where it wants to, and you hear its voice, but do not know where it comes from and where it goes" — the Gospel says (John 3:8). Aside from the physical Berlin Wall, there has always been an invisible line in the heads of most Europeans. We Ukrainians shouldn't get discouraged at their surprise that the European idea, all of a sudden, started "breathing" outside of what was seen as its natural space.

The EU and the West in general have plenty of dilemmas on their plates. They would be glad not to be torn over Ukraine, at least for a while. Or — even better — to find a compromise with Russia. We shouldn't get offended or outraged because of that, either. Our job is to stand our ground and to be patient. But most importantly, our job is to become successful.

Obviously, Ukraine is a big chunk to swallow. It's a large market and the largest country situated entirely in Europe. However, geopolitics cannot be brought down only to economy, demography, geography. It's also about immaterial things. Sometimes primarily so. An idea can bring nations to barricades rather than hunger or profit or fear. It makes nations strong or weak. It either cuts through the walls or creates a mess and makes us regret things for generations. It's a power, a resource, not less vital than oil and gold.

Not long ago, Europe used to have this drive, this inspiration. It got weaker with years, though. Having put "tick" in the "historic unification" box after its two waves of enlargement, the EU was mentally ready to slowly absorb the rest of the Balkans, and focus on other priorities then. The events in Ukraine showed that these plans might need some rethinking. The European idea might have flamed out in some EU parts, but it flamed up in Ukraine. It would be sad if it would burn out for good. It would be a completely different European Union if it would lose its spirit of regional leadership, its zest for life and curiosity about the outside world. When the EU's neighbors raise the European banner on their own, go to war and face death to defend it — aren't you at least curious what happens to them?

In 2013, the European Union went out of its way to ensure that Ukraine is with Europe and that Europe is with Ukraine. The EU was interested, convinced, and principled, while then-president Yanukovych tried to hide his weakness behind "pragmatic" talk. Later, Russia punished Ukraine for her decision to be with Europe by occupying/annexing Crimea and starting the proxy war in Donbas. It turned out that even in the 21st century, one has to pay a terrible price for freedom. It would be sad if now, years into the Euromaidan, the historic tables were to turn, and the EU were to become a kind of collective Yanukovych, hiding its weakness behind lip service to "pragmatism".

Surkov and Emptiness

Darkness can be exciting. Or at least peculiar, as shown by Vladimir Putin's chief strategist Vladislav Surkov, who deserves credit: his manifestos are truly mesmerizing. Especially his last one from 11 February 2019, in the "Nezavisimaya Gazeta."[33] Surkov sounds like a robotic voice from a different world. A world beyond good and evil, morality, and honor. He offers his readers one and only one freedom: freedom from guilt. After all, why should one feel guilty if "it only appears that we have a choice in our doing."[34]

One can condense the Gospel of Surkov into one short idea: the world is darkness (in Russian, it sounds catchier: мир – мрак, *mir – mrak*). He divides the world into two parts: honest and hypocritical. The hypocritical (liberal, western) one hides its true dark nature beyond the "chimeras" of choice, democracy, justice. The honest (Russian) one has cast the chimeras away and embraced its true nature. "Unappealing, but honest".

Yes, Putin's chief strategist, for many years his "brain" in the post-Soviet space, writes it quite unequivocally. It would be plain bizarre and even comical if it weren't so sad. The largest country of the world, the nation that gave the world Tolstoy and Pushkin, has adopted an inhumane, hateful, and primitive doctrine that's hardly comparable to anything else.

I remember a known Russian filmmaker Karen Shakhnazarov paint a surkovesque picture during the "Evening with Vladimir Soloviev", one of Russia's darkest propaganda shows. I couldn't believe my eyes: the film director, whose movies I loved as a teen and who, back in the time, destroyed the lies of the Soviet Union, went on and on about how there is no truth and justice in the world – either in the West or in Russia. Yet, unlike the West, Russia has a "core" that helps it stand straight in this crooked disgusting global reality: Vladimir Putin. And as long as Russia has its beloved

---

33 https://www.ng.ru/ideas/2019-02-11/5_7503_surkov.html
34 This and other Surkov's quotations are from the "Nezavisimaya Gazeta" article above.

leader, as long as it holds on to the "core" ... well, he lost me there. It was kind of blurry what would happen as long as Shakhnazarov did hold on to "the core". I am pretty sure he is blurry about it, too.

The Russian doctrines don't offer any positive agenda aside from rolling back the time to where things were before Gorbachev. What they offer is not a new light, but the old darkness — familiar and cozy. The same one as under Ivan the Terrible, Peter the Great, Lenin. It's Putin's turn now to sell darkness. And he has proved to be a great salesman.

People like myself, who experienced both the Soviet and post-Soviet reality, might have a kind of epiphany comparing the old Soviet thinking and the new Russian one. The Soviets lived under the illusion "we are the good ones — they are the bad ones". Today's Russians live under the illusion "they are the bad ones — so, we must be the bad ones too". This is how things are in the real world. The enemy is at the gate — and it's either them or us.

If you look at it, it's a comfortable choice. It offers the concept of a world with no right or wrong. Why should one even think about it, if (a) "it only appears that we have a choice" and (b) the world is darkness? There is only one thing of importance in this kind of reality: either you win or you lose. And if you are winning, it doesn't matter how: via the covert war in Ukraine, via the use of "Novichok" poison in the UK, via doping at the Olympics, via unleashing malicious propaganda worldwide, or via the bold killings of Putin's adversaries around the globe.

Surkov seems sure Russia is winning. Well, he is partly right. Darkness is on the offensive globally.

The world is getting more and more cynical. The West has less faith in what Surkov calls "chimeras". "Russia Today" has come practically to every Western home. Russian trolls have filled social media. Russia found a perfect and cost-effective way to mess with humanity's head: YouTube, Twitter, Facebook. "Russia gets inside their brain — and they don't know what to do with their changed picture of the world", — Surkov writes in his article. "It results in the paranormal preferences of the electorate. Puzzled and perplexed, they speak of the era of populism. Well, that's one way to describe it, if you don't have other words" — proudly pontificates Putin's grey eminence in his manifesto.

According to Surkov, Russia "anticipated" the dawn of this new brave world. Of course, it's like saying that Jack the Ripper anticipated a spike in London's criminality. Congrats, Jack, you anticipated right! However, wait a minute: getting bigger and spreading "paranormal preferences" among the Western voters — is this Russia's doctrine for years to come? Is that all? Believe it or not, yes.

Russia is good at one thing: destroying and tainting what others have built and believed. Yet, as made so evident in Surkov's text, it doesn't have a positive plan. Surkov mentions "Putinism as the ideology of the future", but doesn't say much about it aside from the assertion that "it needs contemplation and comprehension". In other words, after destroying thousands of lives, they still have to contemplate and comprehend why they did it.

Alas, it's not Surkov's style to "comprehend" or "contemplate" what he did, especially since the real and original Russian doctrine was shaped long before him: "gathering lands". I.e., getting bigger. Through bloodshed, pain, fear, intimidation. Today's Russia doesn't have any idea to offer to the world. America does. Europe does. The Soviet Union did. And Putin's Russia has nothing, aside from its insatiable longing for revenge after the USSR's downfall and aside from its bizarre desire always, at any price, to remain the biggest spot on the world map.

Surkov paints Russia as a trinity, with a relatively reliable "deep people" at the bottom and a state apparatus in the middle, clearly undeserving of Surkov's respect. But he trembles with love and admiration for the one on the top — "the supreme leader". In Surkov's opinion, the Russian state has two functions to fulfill. First, to be "the tool of defense and offense". And second, "to provide a trustful communication and interaction between the supreme leader and the deep people".

And yes, somewhere in-between, there is a niche for the Russian "intelligentsia" — constantly misreading "the deep people" and getting duly punished for it. Probably, like they got punished during the Stalin era.

So much for the "Russian universe". It's a simple reality with a simple set of rules. The most crucial one being (I quote): "Whenever they start building something new in Russia, in the end, they wind up with what used to be, i.e., with what we have." Believe it or not, he brings it up it as a positive thing. I want to believe that it was written by someone not stupid. Maybe even a representative of – dare I say – the "intelligentsia", who initially wanted to change things, but later sold out and came up with this nonsensical ideology cementing and idolizing Russia's sins. A doctrine, so much akin to Mikhail Bulgakov's "empty suit". Well, to be sure, the man is indeed probably not stupid. But his common sense and reason are blinded by his unlimited imperial hubris.

Two things strike you as you read Surkov. First, his audacity. Second, his complete lack of depth. He is all about his trademark extravagant, excessive pride, and this strange, incomprehensible desire "to gather lands". You almost get tempted to read it once again – have I missed something? How could this shallow man, so full of himself, have done so much for promoting the darkness on the planetary scale?

And yet, he has. Of course, Putin isn't just Putin, and Surkov isn't just Surkov. They have an organization, a structure behind them. It was once called "Okhranka" (the "protective police" under the Tsar), "Cheka" (the feared "extraordinary commission" under the Bolsheviks), the notorious NKVD (under Stalin), then KGB. It's called FSB now, "*siloviki*", the secret police, a group of comrades having two things in common: joint enrichment and joint faithfulness to the "supreme leader". They are holding no account to anyone, but him. Putin, Surkov, Ivanov, Shoigu – the names are irrelevant. When the time comes, this womb will bear a new supreme leader with new followership, not better than the current one.

Never in history, there was a power so unlimited (including the power to literally destroy the world) concentrated in the hands so untied. Historically, even in the most cynical states, the government structures had at least one of three limitations: financial, legal or moral. Neither of them applies to Putin's "*siloviki*". They have all the finances, all the military might, and all Russia's oligarchs at their disposal. They ultimately answer only to the "supreme leader". And they see the world along the "they are the bad ones, so we are the bad ones too" maxima.

Sadly, these people are in sync with today's Russia — or, rather, have brought Russia in sync with them. After Crimea, after Donbas and Syria, after Chechnya, after shedding the blood of millions, Putin is joined at the hip with his country, who enthusiastically backed these decisions. It's a bloodline — with the emphasis on "blood". It doesn't come as a surprise that this "group of comrades" is capable to so skillfully manipulate the Russian people. Faced with a binary choice: either you believe that some imaginary enemy is at the gate and that Ukrainians sold out to America, or you admit the truth that Russia has built a "Führer"-led state — Russians choose the bearable lie over the unbearable truth.

The unprecedented concentration of power is multiplied by Russia's insatiable, almost irrational desire for "greatness". And because this hunger isn't sated either by Russia's economic might, or by the happiness of its people, once again — "in the end, they wind up with what used to be, with what we have". In other words, Russia once again measures its greatness in the greatness of its enemies and — of course — in its sheer size, nothing else.

After Yeltsin's short era, there is a steady hand on the Russian political steering wheel. Depending on the situation, this hand can make a fist, be reached out for a handshake — or flip a finger (that was probably the sacral meaning of Surkov's manifesto). Yet, as stated before, there appears one thing this hand can't do: build and create. And if we read Surkov's article right, Putin's state doesn't even aspire to this. Once again, according to Surkov, its primary function is "defense" and "offense". From experience, not necessarily in that order.

Despite all these things, Putin's Russia of the last decades has been diabolically smart on occasion. With the emphasis on "diabolically". They were good at shaping the global narrative, using other nations' weaknesses, sowing doubt, and discord. Time will show what it brings them. This diabolical smartness failed Russia at least twice, in 2004 and 2014. Both times — in Ukraine. And what are all Russia's global gains (real and imaginary) worth, if it has lost what it desired the most? What are all its smarts worth if it misread and misunderstood the nearest and most precious one – Ukraine?

There are two reasons for Russia so deeply misreading Ukraine. The first obvious one is imperial hubris, condescension towards the "peasants" (as they see us Ukrainians). The second one is this: the "world of darkness" theory doesn't really explain Ukraine. Putin honestly tried to intimidate, seduce, or buy Ukraine before attacking it – to no avail. I guess the world is not only darkness, after all. Hey Surkov, where's your sting?

Puzzled and perplexed, Russia decided to declare Ukraine fascist and Russophobe. Well, "that's one way to describe it, if you don't have other words", right, Mr. Grey Eminence? In reality, going through the bloodshed in Ukraine and Syria, through the stolen elections, through the global humiliation of annexations and Russia's constant political saber-rattling, the West develops immunity to this new disease. The disease whose symptoms are so visible in Surkov's writing: dark emptiness, hubris, total lack of empathy posing as "pragmatism". Hopefully, the West will survive and get over it – as it always does. After all, its world perception and historic experience go well beyond "winding up with what used to be" over and over again.

Yes, right now, the West's relation to Russia is akin to a tribe of elves seeking a partner in Mordor. However, the elves too have eyes, common sense, and (who knows!) maybe even some testosterone. And if they see their desired "partner" thinking about heading back to "what used to be", sooner or later it will dawn on them: it's a euphemism for war. The eternal battle between East and West that never stopped raging in the Russian mind. A cold one, a hot one, a holy one, a hybrid one, a propaganda one. Any kind. Russia doesn't see itself outside the concept of the eternal East-West confrontation. The lack of conflict (like in the 1990s) is an insult to Moscow. As they say in Russian jails, "no fear – no respect".

Dear West, if someone is in war-mode against you, you can't call it peace, no matter how badly you try to block things out. And even more so if this someone never stopped being in war-mode. It's one of those notions that are so obvious to Ukraine now, and that will become a painful discovery to the West in the coming years.

After all the excitement about globalization and the new era of international relations, the West will have to "wake up and smell the coffee". The West can reach out a friendly hand over and over again and offer ever new "deals", even (in the worst case) about Ukraine, but in a long run, some kind of a new confrontation paradigm is, unfortunately, inevitable. It's either some kind of confrontation or some kind of capitulation. Russia leaves you no third option.

Mr. Surkov, you can be proud: with your effort and, most importantly, the effort of your "supreme leader", the cold war came back. You are close to rolling back the time, not only nationally, but also globally. With one distinction though: most likely, you won't have the piece of global pie to which you think you are entitled.

Why? Because what you call chimeras (freedom, democracy, human rights) are, in reality, human needs. A kind of essential ones. And if in Kyiv, a city that you dub "Russian Jerusalem", students, teachers, lawyers, workers (Ukraine's "deep people") fight till the end for the sake of what you call chimeras, then … Then your world, your darkness is in danger. If the nations and people do have a choice in their doing (and they do!), your whole world picture will sooner or later fold like an evil house of cards.

And in conclusion, the last thing, from the bottom of my heart. I once met the family of the man who was one of the first victims of Russia's war on Ukraine. Born and bred in Donbas, he was a good-natured civilian who didn't hold a gun and presented no danger to anybody. However, he was openly pro-Ukraine — in those terrible weeks of 2014, when Russia was already on the warpath and Ukraine wasn't. A Russian special-ops group killed, almost sacrificed him with demonstrative, inhuman cruelty. Ever since his family has been without a home. His child screams at night and can't sleep without pills. They lead the painful life of refugees.

Multiply this by hundreds of thousands. This is your life's creation, Mr. Surkov. Yours, your supreme leader's and your deep people's. Add Chechnya and Syria — and you will have millions. Millions of children who scream at night, millions of women who cry into their pillows because of decisions made by you. One day this scream will deafen you.

This is what Russia takes into the future. This is what children and grandchildren of survivors will tell their children and grandchildren in the 22nd century. This is what you take to the other side when the time comes. Of course, if you are right and the world is nothing but darkness, you have nothing to lose. But what if it isn't?

Notes on the Margin of
(Yet Another) Apocalypse

Ukrainian politics can be confusing. This was especially true for Ukraine's 2019 presidential election, with an incumbent Petro Poroshenko being challenged by the actor and comedian Volodymyr Zelenskyi. It had a certain undertone of an Apocalypse. Admittedly, all democratic elections have some of this. The dramatic mood of the end of time is always in the air. Your candidate is always the Messiah. Your opponent is always the Anti-Christ. It's always a life-or-death decision. It's always about avoiding Hell and reaching the Kingdom of Heaven that looms on the horizon. Yet, eventually the voting day comes and goes. Leaflets get thrown into the garbage; yesterday's slogans, wet and lumpy, hang down from the billboards. It's time to get back to normal life. Armageddon can't become your everyday reality.

A democratic election is like a three-tact Vienna waltz: you campaign — you vote — you move on. Ukraine always had a hard time waltzing this third step. Political polarization has been Ukraine's "normal" for quite a while. Yet even by our own extreme measures, today's post-electoral detoxification is especially difficult. The 2019 election is long over — but even amid the pandemic year 2020 it isn't really over. We Ukrainians are stuck in it. To ponder the repercussions, let's take a look at the motivation of the two electoral groups that clashed in this election in a 73%–23% proportion.

The motivation of Petro Poroshenko's 23% was obvious. They voted for the incumbent because in their eyes, he represented two things: (1) Ukraine will be; and (2) Ukraine will be Ukraine. I.e., a nation with her own direction, language, and identity. The Poroshenko voters were fully aware that he wouldn't bring any breakthroughs economically or in any other sense. Yet, they gave him their vote as they saw him as the keeper of the status quo. That was the "knot" of the election, a massive problem for the other aisle of political spectrum. Zelensky's 73% saw "keeping the status-quo" as the worst of all possible outcomes. "Ukraine being Ukraine" didn't sit right with them. They saw it as Ukraine remaining corrupt and stuck in her own political Groundhog Day (with the same faces circulating from one election to another repeatedly).

In the 2019 run-off, Volodymyr Zelensky received the highest credit of trust in Ukraine's history. 73% of the electoral vote. Even Ronald Reagan (to some extent, Zelensky's role model) at his best couldn't dream of such returns. What could have caused this landslide? The answer is banal: people voted for Zelensky because they wanted change. Some for the country—some for themselves individually. Some rationally—some emotionally. Some patriotically and some adolescently. Very different people put very different content into this template. Nothing unusual so far. And yet—why such an impressive outcome?

Maybe, because electoral success isn't about candidates' virtues and flaws, but about their synchronicity with the virtues and flaws of the voters. In other words, having the same virtues and shortcomings as the voter is better for a politician than being "holier than the Pope". Once the voter sees himself in a politician, this politician is unbeatable. Ukraine's "average Joes" saw in Zelensky a reflection of themselves. It was one of those fortuitous moments when the stars were hugely aligned in favor of one of the candidates. After a long line of political creatures who inhabited Ukraine's top political office over nearly 30 years of independence, the country was longing for a human being with whom she would associate herself. Maybe flawed (who isn't?), but relatable.

An election is always, to some degree, a fortuitous moment that extends for years. But let's be honest: as long as we Ukrainians live with a constant feeling of our country being in a freefall, with this permanent sense of Apocalypse in our lives, "agents of change" will always beat the "guarantors of stability" in our elections. That's why, maybe, the Ukrainian word "garant" (a synonym to "president") has this sarcastic, almost derogatory connotation in our political vocabulary. That's why Volodymyr Zelensky, an extremely popular actor, this country's "average Joe" in most of his productions, a man with a good reputation and a sense of humor in real life, was the desired alternative not only to Poroshenko but to the whole history of Ukraine's modern politics. The man with maybe the highest name recognition in the country was out of step with everything in Ukrainian politics—and yet had the guts to stand as a candidate. This combination of courage, celebrity status, and good reputation made people ecstatic.

The history of Ukrainian presidents (with the apparent exception of the exiled Viktor Yanukovych) is simple and somewhat similar. They all came to power convinced that because they were better than their predecessors as people (and of course, this went without saying, the Messiah is always better than the Anti-Christ), they would be better as presidents. Yet relatively soon, it dawned on them that it's not all about their good intentions. The good intentions were there, but the actual change didn't come, and the overall feeling of profound injustice of Ukrainian life stubbornly refused to go away. With time, all accomplishments (even the big ones) faded against the backdrop of this frustrating feeling of collective national failure. This was the moment when most of our presidents, to some extent, morally caved and got frustrated with their own nation. "To keep the boss happy", their teams built an information bubble around them. For a while, it did the job: kept "the boss" happy. Up to the moment when the election came and the bubble burst.

I think, all our presidents got into one and the same labyrinth with the same trap at the end: Ukraine's state apparatus, unchanged, unshaken, unreformed. We have a System (yes, with a capital "S") that warmly embraces every new president, tightens the embrace—and then chokes and swallows him like an anaconda. A System that relentlessly, patriotically, and often selflessly works—for the process, not for the result. A System that drowns the best intentions in a sea of unnecessary words, instructions, clarifications, and decrees. A System that has survived them all and plans to continue to do so.

Ukraine's problem is not that bad state policy was conducted but rather that no state policy was conductible. The state apparatus makes a lot of noise. Yet, in the end, its only result is endless "roadmaps", "working groups", and "action plans". Words, words, words ... If you ever looked for a real "swamp" to drain—there it is. With this quality of most institutions, there was often only one way to accomplish things: circumventing the System via corruption. And because nothing good ever comes out of corruption — as Ukraine's founding father, our first post-Soviet president Leonid Kravchuk formulated it many years ago, "it is what it is" ("*маємо те, що маємо*").

Our presidents all made the same mistake over and over again: tried to solve Ukraine's problems with the help of the System — while the System was Ukraine's #1 problem. At some point, they realized that something was off with Ukraine's state apparatus and tried to reform it. Yet, as made very clear by decades of our history, conducting a reform of the System by the System's rules only makes it stronger.

If I had to pick a mascot for an effective public service reform in a post-Soviet country, I would pick the Grim Reaper. The problem runs so deep that any effective reform must start with fundamentally cleaning house. I.e., with ruining thousands of lives (firing people, bringing to an end their successful careers).

There is a reason why the most effective reformer in the post-Soviet space was also the cruelest — Mikhail Saakashvili, the man who turned hordes of Georgian public servants, many of whom were good people and deserved better, into taxi drivers and pizza delivery boys. The man, who with the same ease broke destinies and rules, even laws. The man, who understandably became the collective object of hate and whose presidency brought him directly to the political abyss. Is there anyone in Ukraine, where everyone owes somebody something, where everybody is somebody's "*koom*,"[35] who would be ready to go this far and to drink from this chalice? I don't see anyone like this on the horizon — and that's Ukraine's big fat minus.

On the other hand, an effective reform means a simultaneous overhaul of both "hardware" and "software". I.e., the new people must come in along with the new technologies of governance. It's easier with technologies than with people. Ukraine has the knowhow to fit our Leviathan (a.k.a. the government) into a

---

35   "Koom" (ukr. «кум») — the godfather of your child or someone, whose child's godfather you are.

smartphone. Ukraine has the specialists knowing how to bring to System what System fears the most: the light, the transparency. This is Ukraine's big fat plus.

And of course, one should be clear that the Leviathan is exceptionally self-sufficient and stable. It never capitulates and rarely collapses. If you want to change things, it probably would make sense not to challenge the Leviathan upfront or wait for it to fall. Re-program it instead — build a system within the System, a pyramid within the pyramid. Lech Walesa did it in Poland in the 1990s. His "pyramid within the pyramid" was the Solidarnosc activists who, placed at all key points of the System, transformed the country and pivoted in the right direction. Vladimir Putin did technically the same in the 2000s — only for an evil purpose. His "pyramid within the pyramid" was his KGB pals from the old times placed at the System's critical corners, and tasked with pivoting Russia in a different direction.

Similarly, it will take mere 100–150 capable state officials and lots of political resolve on the top to transform Ukraine. The question is: do we have this resolve and these people, these "Chicago boys", ready to be honest all the way through and to do what needs to be done. As long as we don't have a clear answer to this question — it's probably to Ukraine's minus. But this can be turned to a plus rather fast. The people are there — you only have to find them, bring them together, motivate and protect from the System.

To reform Ukraine, we need at least some kind of an intermediate solution in Donbas. And for that to happen, we need to be brutally honest and call things by their names. Moreover, we still need to formulate what Ukraine is and what it wants in this world. We should frame it in a way that would resonate both with a Lviv teacher in the West and a Donetsk coal mine worker in the East. We should stop lying to ourselves and our people. If we are so keen on saying the truth (and judging from the Facebook battles among various factions of the Ukrainian population, we are!), let's shine the light of truth at ourselves first and only after that on the others.

The bloodshed in Donbas won't stop as long as we don't make peace with the idea that a part of our territory is under Russian occupation for a long haul, and we can't liberate it militarily. No, we will never accept the occupation legally or politically, de-facto or de-jure, we will never denounce what is legally and lawfully ours, but getting our land back will be a long and tiresome process. Acknowledging this fact would imply, in my opinion, that we need a new fundament and new philosophy of the peace process in the Minsk framework—or instead of it.

The philosophy of the Minsk agreements was based on the notion that all sides wanted peace. It's obvious now (and, quite frankly, was obvious when the agreements were concluded) that what Russia wants is not peace, but control over Ukraine. Bestowing Russian passports on the population of Donbas and Crimea in 2014–2019 was the cementation of the occupation. It showed that "Minsk" was only partly an instrument of peace, but partly—a mirage, an illusion.

"Minsk" fulfilled its function both for Kyiv (as it quelled the bleeding) and for Moscow (as it let Russia fully stretch its tentacles into occupied territory). But "Minsk" alone won't solve the problem for Ukraine and won't even stop the bleeding altogether. To reach this goal, one needs to think in a different timeframe than we have so far. It's a painful truth, but it needs to be told—to Ukraine, to Ukraine's friends abroad, and, most importantly, to those who hurt the most: the people who left their homes and a part of their lives under the occupation.

As long as Crimea and a part of Donbas are under occupation, Russia will remain the enemy. Moscow made this decision on its own, when it conducted and celebrated Crimea's "liberation" from Ukraine. When one nation's biggest triumph becomes the biggest humiliation of the other, this kind of historic trauma doesn't just go away. It leaves scars, brings a tectonic shift, that will be our reality for decades to come. On the other hand, we need to learn how to live next to an enemy without being constantly at war. And we need to learn that now. All Ukraine's intellectual and diplomatic potential should be focused on this: bringing about peace without bringing about a capitulation.

"Each European democratic state can become a member of EU",—says "Kinderlexicon", the German-language encyclopedia for children that I keep reading with my daughter before bed. This is essential, elementary. And yet, even though Ukraine is both European and democratic, her European or Euro-Atlantic perspective isn't something that's being seriously discussed. This sobering truth has to do not only with the fact that Europe is going through a rough patch right now, but also with the fact that the project of European unity is primarily the project of trust. As I mentioned before, Ukraine has some work to do to that end.

Becoming a part of a United Europe means becoming a part of the circle of trust. Ukraine will be seriously considered as an eventual member of this space when Ukraine is trusted. This won't happen sooner than we Ukrainians

1. start trusting each other,
2. start believing in our own country, and
3. start believing in Europe as it is and not as we imagine it to be.

And because these three domestic goals aren't within reach yet, it would be honest to ponder two things: first—there is no alternative to Ukraine being with Europe; and second—a formal EU perspective isn't something worth claiming or even mentioning till we get our ducks in a row.

NATO membership is a different story. If the EU is a project of trust, NATO is the project of courage. I see in Ukraine the courage to enter NATO, but I don't see in NATO so far, the courage to accept Ukraine as a member. And that's something we need to be honest about, too. It's not true that Ukraine joining the EU and NATO depends 100% on us. I'd rather say it's 50% on us and 50% on many other aspects of European and international life. To use poetic language, the stars must align, domestically, and internationally. They haven't so far.

Summing up, Ukraine needs three things to become a better nation. First, change the mood in the country, shrug off this constant apocalyptic feeling in our daily lives. It's not good for the nervous system of a nation to live with a sense of a constant freefall. Second, get a hold over the state apparatus—Ukraine's key domestic problem. Make it work for the result and not for the process. Third, end the Donbas war without sacrificing Ukraine's freedom.

Those are three conundrums, three herculean tasks, three goals Ukraine needs to master. We might be closer to it than one would imagine. It's a matter of time (and of political resolve, communication skills, convincing power, right management) till we do it. Admittedly, it's not a small endeavor, but it's doable.

What Will Bring Peace to Ukraine's Soul?

From a historical perspective, Ukraine's existence is an existence between worlds. We were constantly seen and treated not as an entity but as a territory, "lands", space, ground for something. Napoleon's entourage played with the idea of creating here a new state named "Napoleonida". Hitler planned to resettle to Ukraine a "racially superior genetic stock" in place of the Slavic "Untermenschen". Stalin kneaded Ukrainians like bloody play-dough under his knuckles. We lived on these "lands", but were invisible. Our work made others rich. Our talent made others proud. Our fields fed others. Our spirit was enslaved. Our culture was on the way to becoming nothing but an ethnic eccentricity. Our language was on the path to becoming nothing but an accent.

We shouldn't have existed by now. We should have been dissolved in others. And yet, this didn't happen. Whenever some historic monster brought Ukraine to the brink of non-existence, it was the monster who ceased to exist, not Ukraine. That's what happened with the Russian Tsar Empire. That's what happened with the Soviet Union. It's as if history didn't want us to vanish and gave us one chance after another – and we squandered them all. Of course, every time that happens, we have a solid explanation. Mostly, we blame our misfortunes on those who should be our highest authority – the Ukrainian people. We, the elite, are good and progressive – they, the people, are bad and backwards.

Ukraine is like a river with two sides. On the one side (let's call it the "riverside A") we have the part of the elite – both Ukrainian-, and Russian-speaking – that doesn't see itself apart from Ukraine. On the other side (let's call it the "riverside B"), we have Ukraine's anti-elite. Smart, well-educated, mostly Russian-speaking people for whom Ukrainian statehood is nothing but an unfortunate accident, a bunch of peasants thinking too much of themselves. Geopolitically, they see Ukraine as Russia's underbelly. Culturally, they see Ukraine as an ethnographic curiosity, nothing more.

Between these two extremes, between devotion and contempt there is a whole stream of life – human masses, people, whose attitude to their country is a point between A and B. Their country is a part of them, but not "above everything". As for most people in the world, actually.

These "masses", this enigmatic "electorate" — this is the real Ukraine. Simple people, whose "above everything" is how to feed their family and raise their children, survive in a world of viruses, tumors, and heart attacks, make a living, and find a drop of national comfort in a whole sea of talk about doom-and-gloom.

Ukraine's anti-elite is a topic for a separate publication. Its goal is to bring Ukraine back under Russia's shadow. Its political thinking is on display in the Russian daily political TV shows, where Ukraine is traditionally the #1 item and where "pro-Russian Ukrainian politicians" are always welcomed guests. Other than that, the anti-elite is a static entity, like a malign bacterium, that can spend a lifetime dormant in the human body and be "activated" only when the right moment comes. However, let's focus now on those whose function is to make sure that this "right moment" never arrives. I.e. — on Ukraine's true elite, the "riverside A". The educated, inspired, and patriotic Ukrainians (no matter of what ethnic heritage).

Ukrainian statehood was built around and brought about by those who believed in Ukraine. After centuries of the nation's quasi-existence, there weren't too many of those in the beginning, in the late 1980s and early 1990s. But their number rose with years. They brought up a whole generation of those who see Ukraine's future in and with Europe. They made sure that the Ukrainian language didn't die out, and the culture wasn't reduced to mere "ethnography". They are the Biblical "yeast" that worked through the dough of the Ukrainian nation.

The elite's function in Ukraine was, first, to build a political nation and, second, to lead it. Well, the nation has been built. If not completely, then at least in general, most important features. Ukraine's idea is firmly ensconced with the minds of the young, politically active, and dynamic. Yet, it turned out that out our elite had a harder time with its second function: leading ahead.

In our desires and declarations, we are firmly with Europe, but in our essence, we are often still stuck with the sins of our post-

Soviet past. Not only the sins of the flesh (like corruption, for instance) but also the sins of the spirit. I mean primarily the sin of doublethink. We are too often pro-European, but against tolerance, feminism, respect for minorities, and the freedom of speech for those who disagree with us. I.e.—against what today's Europe stands for.

Too often, we are for Europe and against it at the same time. Too often, we are annoyed by democracy and freedom, although—paradoxically enough—we pay for them a higher price than any other nation. Too often, we forget that Europe is more than just a desire to move away from Moscow and from the communist past. It's a political language, a set of values, of norms of behavior—all those things on which we still have to work.

Right after Russia attacked us in 2014, there was a moment when it seemed like a new countdown started in Ukraine's history. Thousands of people took to the front to defend their country. From that heroic moment on, our independence wasn't just a gift of history, but a result of the unthinkable sacrifice on the part of thousands of Ukrainians. Yet, even this didn't calm our national soul. Thousands went to war, millions volunteered for and donated to the army, but this didn't answer the question that has been haunting us through decades: "What is it that makes us, with all our diversity, one nation under God?"

Why didn't this country, so diverse and filled with self-doubt, fall apart in the direst of the times? Why didn't her people turn away from her? Why didn't the idea of Ukraine as a "failed nation" (for years promoted by Russia) take root in Ukrainian minds and souls? With all that we have learned about Ukrainians during the war—aren't we too hasty to blame Ukraine's misfortune on the "masses"? Maybe, instead of loving them in the good times and hating in the bad, we should accept them as a higher authority and try to understand what is essential for them. Maybe, we should try to educate them and sometimes (sorry for the heretical thought!) *learn* from them.

In 2014, Ukraine didn't fall. And today, once again, she asks: "Now what?". A friend of mine, a good and cheerful man, has been in a deep depression for quite a while because "Ukraine voted for the wrong one" in the 2019 election. He is still patriotic, he still can't see himself apart from Ukraine, but in his mind, his beloved country started existing apart from the people inhabiting it. He still believes in Ukraine, but he somehow stopped believing in Ukrainians. And he isn't the only one whose soul split after the electoral battles of 2019.

Theodor Herzl allegedly once said it takes a great enemy to create a great nation. On March 18th, 2014, the infamous final day of Crimea annexation, this great enemy emerged officially, on a constitutional level. Putin stole Crimea and changed the Russian constitution to make the steal as irreversible as possible. Countries that steal your land can't be your friends; annexations make normal relations impossible—that's the inevitable fact that marks Ukrainian lives ever since.

The Crimean betrayal was a shock and a slap in the face for some Ukrainians—and a logical, expected continuation of the Ukraine-Russia historic enmity for the others. The year 2014 united those who "always knew" and those who "nevertheless believed" (that Ukraine and Russia could get along). There was a third category too: those who rooted for Putin, but as they were in a clear minority, let's leave them out for a moment. I'm talking about the two categories of Ukrainian patriots who found themselves in one and the same virtual (or sometimes real) war trench. In 2014, we all got attacked, offended, and slandered by Russia.

I'll never forget Russia's former film director, an Academy Award winner and now full-time Putin propagandist Nikita Mikhalkov asking in one of his TV shows a rhetorical question: why didn't Russian-speaking Ukrainians of the East and South enthusiastically rise in support of the so-called "Russian spring"? His explanation fit nicely into Mikhalkov's understanding of what moves people: "They simply got scared!" In reality, Ukrainians of the East and South didn't support Putin for the simple reason that they are Ukrainians. No matter what ethnicity, language, or level of "national consciousness", Ukraine is their country. If you attack Ukraine, if you come like a thief in the night and steal another nation's land, you forfeit your right to any "spring".

A new feeling imbued many of us in those months of 2014 — the sense of a common Ukrainian family. A feeling that seemed both exhilarating and transformational. It gave new hope in a time of despair. Yet later on (to borrow a phrase from an old Soviet film), "it shrank and shrank, till it got tiny like a kidney stone."[36] At some point, we, once again, descended into a new national quarrel. A tough and brutal one, even by our measures. Divided into pro- and contra-Poroshenko, we banned and blocked each other on social media. We became each other's enemies — sometimes even worse enemies than the one who stole our land. It was a bitter moment. After all, why should the enemy even need a war, if we are doing his job, battling each other verbally on a daily basis?

This might be the most dangerous moment in our newest history. Even more dangerous than the year 2014. Countries vanish not when they get attacked, but when their citizens stop believing in them. In 1941–1945, Hitler couldn't beat the Soviet Union — and just 50 years later, the Soviet Union died on its own, without any outside threat or attack, as it became the embodiment of everything failing, retrograde and backward in the eyes of its citizens. Back then, any alternative seemed better than this dull, inferior, awkward kingdom of routinely dying general secretaries. And yes, at that point, one push was enough for the whole huge construction to crumble.

Admittedly, our Ukrainian "general secretaries" don't die. We routinely throw them to the political dump — figuratively and sometimes literally. Year after year, our political system grows more and more toxic. After each election, we have a harder and harder time detoxing and returning to everyday life. As stated earlier, in 2019, we did not detox at all. The 2019 election still rages on in Ukrainian heads.

After each election, there is a chance to heal and reunite. There was one after 2019, too. There appears to be none today, though. Not with today's political actors and parties. We became estranged as a nation — seriously and for long. One group will be for Zelensky, the other — for Poroshenko. One group will continue demanding

---

36 https://en.wikipedia.org/wiki/The_Meeting_Place_Cannot_Be_Changed

peace with Russia, the other — victory over Russia and forceful de-occupation of Crimea and a part of Donbas. The question is how soon this feud will be over and whether we'll pay for it with our statehood.

The enemy who attacked us and made us bleed isn't on the edge of our emotions anymore. His place was taken by the most hideous, disgusting category of human beings — Ukrainians who disagree with us and vote against our candidates. Our souls are filled with despair and aggression. We can't remember the last time when we said something good about our own country. And yes, this is the path to the kind of situation when one push would be enough for the whole construction to crumble.

If we have a constant stream of dirt instead of a civilized democratic discourse, if there is nothing but bitterness in our political conversations, if Maidan, Maidan, and Maidan once again is our universal solution to the gridlocks of Ukrainian politics — there is a possibility that in the end, we'll do our enemy's job for him. I.e. disgust Ukrainians with Ukraine, convince ourselves that we are indeed a failed nation. We might drown our country in our own bile. Let's not let this happen!

"Now is the worst that has ever been" — this is a phrase I have heard my whole life. Ukrainians as a nation live longer, dress better, travel more, look healthier — but this phrase doesn't go away. Emotionally, we are like Alice in Wonderland, falling into our imaginary black hole. In our own eyes, we are the poorest and unhappiest in the world. For some reason, we find comfort pitying ourselves like that.

Still, why is it getting so dark now? What has changed in 2019–2020? What is new in our "Wonderland"? Is the government making mistakes? Well, they always do. Is Russia winning? Not really — at least judging from what you hear at the Russian talk shows and from pro-Russian voices in Ukraine. In reality, neither the elite, nor the anti-elite, nor Putin, nor anyone else can change who we are, our essence, the free choice between good and bad that we make daily and hourly. Ukraine, in her current condition, is a product of at least three decades of independence. And no government — good or bad — can change it within months or even years.

What's new is the elite losing its faith in its people. The bright ones went dark. The salt stopped being salty. The "riverside A", whose enthusiasm was holding Ukraine afloat for years, started seeing Ukrainians as "Putin's useful idiots" because they voted for Volodymyr Zelenskyi. The true elite started talking about their nation with almost as much vitriol as Russia and the pro-Russian forces in Ukraine.

Needless to say, this might cause a major disintegration from within. Once there is no sense of "gravity" anymore on the part of the nation's best, what is left to hold us Ukrainians together?

The elite at odds with its own people is akin to a head at odds with its body. Paradoxically enough, it's nothing new, either. This virus has been raging through the world for quite a while, infecting different countries differently. The "forgotten" Americans, British, Brazilians (the list can go on much longer) vote for the "wrong ones", and the elite finds nothing better but to blame its people for its own inability to find a way to the hearts and minds of the masses. It's a global phenomenon: the bright and smart can't reach the rest of society. Either they don't find the right words, or maybe—just maybe!—the elites have to work on their communication skills. "In the beginning, was the Word"—and what was in the end?

Maybe, in the end, there was Twitter and Facebook. The elite (both in and outside Ukraine) clearly wasn't ready for social media to dominate the global discourse. In place of the world of printed or televised media, whose attention and voice had to be deserved or could be bought, came a world dominated by social media where everyone has a voice. The political discourse became somewhat akin to a bird colony that quickly gets hysterical and hateful. This world is often deaf to reason. It's a world where simple answers "out-scream" common sense. And simple answers can be dangerous.

Fascism was a prominent example of a simple answer that gets ahold of the mass consciousness. Back in time, Adolf Hitler told Germans that Jews were to blame for their problems—and Germans liked the explanation. Nowadays, social media offers a more comprehensive range of those to blame: political opponents, liberals, ethnic minorities, deep state, George Soros, etc. Facebook and

Twitter became a virtual ray of death, easily utilized to deafen reason and burn out dissent. It's a potent weapon in the hands of politicians and manipulators. Everyone likes getting "likes" and "retweets". No one wants to be insulted and hated.

The humankind in general and Ukraine, in particular, got separated by social media into herds, echo chambers. The first commandment of political communication became "stick with your herd", do and say what your echo chamber is obsessed with — or keep it shut. Where is the national and global interest or mere common sense in this sea of overblown, constantly screaming egos? There is none.

These are angry, loud times. They will end when our "bird colony" learns to think before screaming and when the people will finally hear the elite (and vice versa). It's a test for our society's ability to grow up. The elite must grow up in one way, and the people — in another. The head/body conflict must stop. Nationally and globally. Maybe someday, the elite (Ukrainian and international) will learn to use the new media to speak to the masses, appealing to the best and not to the worst in them. I am convinced: Twitter and Facebook can be more than a political ray of death.

Maybe, someday, when God Almighty once again saves Ukraine and the world (this time from the coronavirus), there will be a time for sobering and reckoning. Maybe at some point, the ways of the elites and the masses will cross offline. They will look each other in the eye and think of the old simple commandment: love your neighbor as yourself. And maybe that will be the moment when we look at ourselves, think of our words and deeds, of all the screaming and quarrelling to which we (as individuals, as a nation, as humankind) have sunk in recent years — and feel ashamed. And maybe, who knows, this feeling of shame could be the beginning of a new time for all of us.

Epilogue

For Ukrainians who were born in the 1970s in the Soviet Union, life was anything but boring. In fact, more than on one occasion it was a real emotional roller coaster. At first, you get born into the Soviet reality and spend enough years in it to absorb at least some of what Soviet propaganda was teaching and preaching—just to realize: it was all a lie. Then you get the historic privilege to see Ukraine become independent. You even get to co-create this independence—just to see the irresponsible and incapable post-communist elite hijack your newly created independent country and loot it for years. Then you see something most of us thought was unthinkable—a Ukrainian revolution, the ordinary people rising for freedom and justice. Not even once, but twice—in 2004 and in 2013–2014.

Then Putin annexed Crimea and started his hideous, duplicitous, undeclared war in Donbas. Seven years into the war, I see three plagues befall Ukraine: Putin, the COVID-19 pandemic and the unprecedented political polarization. Three decades of freedom and democracy have changed Ukraine profoundly, but haven't made her much happier. Amazingly, the world around us, including the nations that we see as our etalon, slowly descends into an atmosphere of self-doubt, moral weakness and quarrel, too. We see it in America, but also in Europe. Unfreedom is on the march.

Putin's Russia avails itself on every opportunity to "divide and conquer" the outside world. Opportunities are abundant. Russian government believes, wishes and preaches via state propaganda that the modern civilization comes—more or less—to some kind of a reboot. They seem convinced the dollar-based global economy will inevitably collapse, leading to a major global shake-up which will create what Russia longs for: a new economic beginning, new growth space for nations that have "what really matters"—oil and weapons. Incapable to catch up with other big nations, Russia wishes for the world to reset. Well, you may like it or not, but it's a strategy. They split the West, fill it with doubt and self-deprecation. Incapable of challenging the enemy economically or militarily, they weaken him morally—in the hope that he doesn't defend himself.

What's the push-back? I don't see much of it so far. Who is the moral leader to call things by their name and say the right words to the West's exasperated societies and lead by example? I see none. Western politicians live from election to election. Some of them (let's be honest) look with inferiority complex at Putin who survived them all and, apparently, plans to do so indefinitely.

Modern religion, instead of leading, undergoes an even deeper crisis than modern politics. One part of the church is quietly losing the ground under its feet — with thinning parishes and disillusioned, "cell"-centered youth. The other one firmly, blindly adores Trump, Putin and other decision-makers, whoever decides to give the church financial benefits. With this kind of leadership, the line between good and evil can water down rather fast.

As a faithful Christian, it hurts me to see the Western world like this. Post-truth means truthless; truthless means godless. For me, United Europe has always been the fulfillment of Christ's two basic ideas: forgiveness (in this case, historical) and humility (in this case, of those at power). I see Christianity as the key to Europe's miracle and success. I also don't see the Western tolerance culture as something contradicting the teaching of Christ (but that's probably a topic to another book). When I see a pastor's daughter Angela Merkel, the most powerful woman on earth, year after year take a low-cost plane to a low-cost vacation — I understand what Fukuyama meant by the "end of history". What can be more reassuring in terms of seeing the positive future for the mankind than a leader with this level of dedication, self-restraint and humility?

So, how can this part of the world go post-truth so precipitously? Why aren't moral politicians taking the lead when it's needed the most? How could the world based on ideas of forgiveness and humility all of a sudden become so accepting of the world of revanchism and shameless corruption? More concretely: what makes the West so stubbornly shake Putin's blood-stained hands and try to find a spark of hope for the world in his dead eyes? Money can't be the sole explanation. Neither can be the naivete of the western elites. Nor the fear of Putin doing something insane on a global scale. Nor the deceptive notion of having "so much in common" with today's Russia. But maybe if you put all these factors together, you'll get close to explaining why the refined and civilized West looks so weak in the face of defiant and impudent Putin.

Democracy is a reality based on the assumption that human beings are good by their nature, and therefore, if you give them freedom, positive things come out of it. Dictatorships, on the other hand, predicate on the assumption that human beings, wicked by their nature, can't be trusted with freedom, because they'll inevitably abuse it. This explains the striking difference between the trail left in the history by the democratic world and the world of dictatorships. One part of the world believes in the good in people; the other one — in the bad in them.

When I walk along Vienna streets, there are many things that I see — good or bad. But most importantly, I see ... love. Love of those who live here. Love to what you do. Love to where you live. And yes, there is no shame in admitting it — love to yourself. From this vantage point, it's almost impossible to imagine that somewhere, not far from this wonderful place, there is someone who would want to question this idyll, challenge and subjugate it. J.R.R. Tolkien parallels rush to mind rather instantly. Valinor needs Mordor as a partner, wants to shake hands with Sauron. And all Mordor wants is having his part of the "global pie" back.

For instance, he wants my town: Kyiv. Torn, disillusioned, but unbroken. When I walk the streets of my town, I see many things as well, but, for the most part, love isn't one of them. First of all, I see ... tiredness. Tiredness of the daily need to survive. Tiredness of injustice. Tiredness of being poor. We Ukrainians come from an unfreedom-filled past. Unfreedom leaves little space for love. Time and again, revolution after revolution, Ukrainians want to break out of this loveless reality. Unsuccessfully so far. Incapable of escaping it, many decide to emigrate. And yet Ukraine is not through with her dream of becoming a better nation. The European idea is changing Ukraine from within. Like the proverbial yeast it's still working through the dough — and we haven't seen the last of it yet. With support of the free world, we can and must turn the corner. The free world has a vested interest: too many things depend on whether Ukraine succeeds.

The revanchist Russia wants not only to reshape the post-Soviet space, but revert history in general. It wants to roll back the clock. The success or failure of creating USSR 2.0 hangs on Ukraine. In view of Russia's onslaught on the West and its attempt to reclaim the Russia-controlled part of the world, the mankind split into three groups. First, those who don't care—or even think Russians are entitled to having what is "theirs". Second, those who believe in freedom, and think that zones of influence belong in the same dustbin of history as slavery and colonialism. Third, those whom Russia wants to control again: primarily the former nations of the USSR. Ukraine's answer to Putin's dreams is loud and clear: no, we won't move back. We aren't Mordor. We don't want to be Mordor. We'll never be Mordor.

Nothing will change this. The idea of Ukraine as a part of "Russian world" has sailed with the last Ukrainian military vessels leaving the occupied Crimea in 2014. Understanding this, Putin wants to break Ukraine, push her to the floor, make an example out of her for others who want freedom. That's what today's fight is about. Now, pick your side in it. Which of the three groups do you belong to?

I know that many my compatriots will have a bone to pick with me after reading this book. Probably, many bones. But primarily about my idea that Ukraine is a nation that, paradoxically enough, outgrew her elite; and that the elite, the educated and empowered, is to blame for Ukraine's failures, rather than impoverished and less educated masses. My opponents would probably argue, an elite is never better or worse than the nation, but an exact reflection of it. "Every nation deserves its government". Which usually makes sense. But not in Ukraine's case. Two revolutions within one decade showed: Ukraine wants better and deserves better. The fact that the very dream for which people twice went to barricades didn't come true, has to do with those whose job is to represent people: politicians, elite.

The thing with the elite is that it can change quicker than the masses—once the time is right and the person is there to plough through. I wish Ukraine's political class was the factor of change and not cementing Ukraine's sins. It's not quite the case yet, but, despite the wide-spread misconception, Ukraine's face-off with Putin is expediting the birth of a new elite, not slowing it down.

Was Vaclav Havel the reflection of Czechoslovakia, when he came to power? Probably not. But he changed things profoundly, pulled the nation ahead. Who is the true reflection of Germany and its elite — the moral and dedicated Angela Merkel or her predecessor Gerhard Schroeder who so shamelessly sold out for Russian money? Hard to tell, but Angela Merkel surely pulls the nation ahead, whereas the schroeders of this world make many Germans just as ashamed as many Ukrainian politicians make Ukraine.

My country is still waiting for her Vaclav Havel or Angela Merkel — and the time will come. That's why I don't just blame Ukraine's elite for the nation's misfortunes, but also pin my hopes on it. Ukraine is still young. We are still growing up. We are still learning things. In the last years, we learned to defend ourselves, to stand our ground — that's a big one. Now we have to learn to believe in ourselves and shrug off what holds us back.

Ukraine's story hasn't been told yet. The outcome will give direction to the whole post-Soviet region. Maybe beyond. During my diplomatic career, I heard so many stories of leaders of the post-Soviet space, publicly close to Putin, whispering to Ukraine's leaders: "Don't mind what we say publicly. We root for you. If you are toast, we are toast, either". Of course, after this, they probably whispered something completely different in Putin's ear, and nevertheless, it reveals Putin's key problem: In the end of the day, people with a choice don't want to live in his "Russian world".

Some want to make money off it. Some like to spend money in it. Some want to indulge in sins rejected in the West, but tolerated or even embraced in Russia (racism, homophobia, sexism, nationalism …). However, being a part of Russian world isn't what people wish for themselves and especially their children. Even Snowden wants out. Even the most stubborn putinista see the creation of their president as an ugly necessity, the lesser of the evils, but not the ultimate good. That's why President Trump's claim America isn't much better than Russia, when it comes to killing people (remember his infamous 2017 FoxNews interview with Bill O'Reilly?[37]) was such a

---

37   https://edition.cnn.com/2017/02/04/politics/donald-trump-vladimir-putin/index.html

blow. Keeping up the West's self-doubt is Putin's one and only chance to reach his goals. All Putin needs to do is feed it, keep it alive. If the self-doubt is there — the West's foreign policy will boil down to a reset after a reset after a reset. The West will keep "giving diplomacy a chance", while Putin will keep giving a chance to his bombers, special-op groups and professional poisoners.

In my humble opinion, the most important thing the West needs to do, is finally give a simple answer: "Yes, we are better than them". Because freedom is better than unfreedom. Because we don't bomb and poison people for their desire to be free. And if someone does, if someone fights against freedom, then we fight back. The time for a compromise and a (proper) reset might come in the future. But today is the time to stand for what you are and what you believe in.

Democracy and freedom, American dream and European idea are the best thing the mankind came up with so far politically. Without these concepts, the world would be what it used to be a hundred and five hundred years ago: a bunch of superpowers carving up the globe like a turkey, over and over again. American dream and European idea, United Europe and idealistic America is a historic accomplishment of the whole mankind. The West in general and United Europe in particular give hope for a new, better reality not only to Americans and Europeans, but to all people of good will around the world, to those who value freedom and are tired of unfreedom. Accordingly, giving up the West's ideals, playing the "pragmatism" game with dictators of this world, would mean giving up not only on the West, but on the mankind.

UKRAINIAN VOICES

Collected by Andreas Umland

The book series "Ukrainian Voices" publishes English- and German-language monographs, edited volumes, document collections, and anthologies of articles authored and composed by Ukrainian politicians, intellectuals, activists, officials, researchers, and diplomats. The series' aim is to introduce Western and other audiences to Ukrainian explorations, deliberations and interpretations of historic and current, domestic, and international affairs. The purpose of these books is to make non-Ukrainian readers familiar with how some prominent Ukrainians approach, view and assess their country's development and position in the world. The series was founded and the volumes are collected by Andreas Umland, Dr. phil. (FU Berlin), Ph. D. (Cambridge), Associate Professor of Politics at the Kyiv-Mohyla Academy and Senior Expert at the Ukrainian Institute for the Future in Kyiv.

SOVIET AND POST-SOVIET POLITICS AND SOCIETY

Editor: Andreas Umland

Founded in 2004 and refereed since 2007, SPPS makes available affordable English-, German-, and Russian-language studies on the history of the countries of the former Soviet bloc from the late Tsarist period to today. It publishes between 5 and 20 volumes per year and focuses on issues in transitions to and from democracy such as economic crisis, identity formation, civil society development, and constitutional reform in CEE and the NIS. SPPS also aims to highlight so far understudied themes in East European studies such as right-wing radicalism, religious life, higher education, or human rights protection.

JOURNAL OF SOVIET AND POST-SOVIET POLITICS AND SOCIETY

Editor: Julie Fedor

The Journal of Soviet and Post-Soviet Politics and Society was launched in April 2015 as a bi-annual companion journal to the Soviet and Post-Soviet Politics and Society book series (founded in 2004 and edited by Andreas Umland, Dr. phil., Ph.D.). Like the book series, the journal provides an interdisciplinary forum for original research on the Soviet and post-Soviet world. The journal strives to publish creative, intelligent, and lively writing, which tackles and illuminates significant issues and is capable of engaging wider educated audiences beyond the academy.

ibidem
Press

BALKAN POLITICS AND SOCIETY

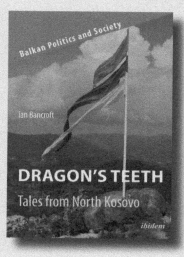

Editors: Jelena Džankić, Soeren Keil

The book series Balkan Politics and Society (BPS), launched in 2018, focuses on original empirical research on understudied aspects of the multifaceted historical, political, and cultural trajectories of the Balkan region. The series includes:
- Discussions on the political systems of the Balkan states, including single country case studies and comparative research
- Analyses of relevant policy fields
- Studies of the link between contemporary political issues and historical debates
- Historical debates on the Balkan states
- Analyses of the social and economic reality of the region
- Research on the evolution and development of different cultures in the region
- Discussions on the evolution of the various societies in the Balkan

FORUM FÜR OSTEUROPÄISCHE IDEEN- UND ZEITGESCHICHTE

Editors: Leonid Luks, Gunter Dehnert, Alexei Rybakow, Andreas Umland

FORUM is a bi-annual journal featuring interdisciplinary discussions on the history of ideas. It showcases studies by political scientists, philosophers as well as literary, legal, and economic scholars, and books reviews on Central and Eastern European history. The journal offers critical insight into scientific discourses across Eastern Europe to Western readers by translating and publishing articles by Russian, Polish, and Czech researchers.

ibidem Press | Leuschnerstr. 40 | 30457 Hannover | Germany
Phone: +49 (0) 511 2 62 22 00 | Fax: +49 (0) 511 2 62 22 00 | sales@ibidem.eu

Literature and Culture in Central and Eastern Europe

Editor: Reinhard Ibler

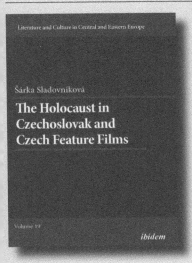

The book series Literature and Culture in Middle and Eastern Europe aims to provide a forum for current research on literature and culture in Central and Eastern Europe. It prioritizes a spatial-regional concept over a purely philological one, e.g. Slavic, in order to better reflect the numerous interrelationships that characterize the literature and cultures of Eastern Central, Southeastern and Eastern Europe as well as the German-speaking world. The series aims to uncover these manifold mutual contacts, overlaps, and influences, both individually and as a whole.

Journal of Romanian Studies

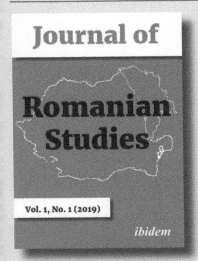

Editors: Peter Gross, Svetlana Suveica and Iuliu Ratiu

The *Journal of Romanian Studies*, jointly developed by The Society for Romanian Studies and ibidem Press, is a biannual, peer-reviewed, and interdisciplinary journal. It examines critical issues in Romanian studies, linking work in that field to wider theoretical debates and issues of current relevance, and serving as a forum for junior and senior scholars. The journal also presents articles that connect Romania and Moldova comparatively with other states and their ethnic majorities and minorities, and with other groups by investigating the challenges of migration and globalization and the impact of the European Union.

ibidem Press